THE ENGLISH-TEACHING LIBRARY

The Teaching of Structural Words and Sentence Patterns

STAGE 3

BY

A. S. HORNBY

LONDON
OXFORD UNIVERSITY PRESS
1962

Oxford University Press, Amen House, London E.C.4

GLASGOW   NEW YORK   TORONTO   MELBOURNE   WELLINGTON
BOMBAY   CALCUTTA   MADRAS   KARACHI   LAHORE   DACCA
CAPE TOWN   SALISBURY   NAIROBI   IBADAN   ACCRA
KUALA LUMPUR   HONG KONG

PRINTED IN GREAT BRITAIN BY HEADLEY BROTHERS LTD
109 KINGSWAY LONDON WC2 AND ASHFORD KENT

CONTENTS

CONTENTS

CONTENTS

INTRODUCTION

STAGE THREE of this series sets out more teaching items of the kind dealt with in *Stage One* and *Stage Two*. Almost all the teaching items which are to be found in the syllabuses published during recent years for the teaching of English as a foreign language are dealt with in these three books. Items not yet dealt with are those not suitable for oral presentation and oral drills, for example, the problems of reported (or indirect) speech, and non-defining (or non-restrictive) relative clauses. These need to be dealt with through written exercises, not by means of oral drills. Methods for presenting these items will be discussed in another book in this *English-Teaching Library*. There will be suggestions for designing and using suitable exercises.

With *Stage Three* it becomes even more difficult, but also less important and less necessary, to arrange teaching items in the order in which they are likely to occur in textbooks. There is some unanimity on the order of teaching items in the beginning stage. As the English course advances there is likely to be increasing divergence. Some textbook writers, perhaps influenced by local examination requirements, will give prominence to reported speech in the third year; others will limit their illustration of this feature to quite simple examples.

With *Stage Three* it becomes more necessary for the teacher to use his own judgement on what items deserve time and attention, and on what items may be dealt with briefly. The teacher has to decide which items need oral presentation and oral drills, and which items are best dealt with in the mother tongue. Vocabulary items are an obvious example. Many new words and phrases will occur. Are these to be identified by the use of demonstration procedures (drawings, pictures, activities, etc.), by contextual procedures, or by giving the equivalent in the mother tongue (or by requiring pupils to use a dictionary)?

The items chosen for inclusion in *Stage Three* are, for the most part, those for which demonstration or contextual procedures are possible. This does not mean, however, that the mother tongue is never to be used. It may often be a useful and economical starting-point. The difference between *may not* and *must not*, for which examples (as given in §§ 124) are necessary, may also be given by means of translation. It is important to present the verb *wish* (dealt with in Chapter Sixteen) by means of numerous examples. It may also be useful, even necessary, to compare *wish* and *want* with those verbs in the language of your pupils that cover approximately the same area of meaning.

Stage Three gives occasional warnings that a teaching item may be presented and illustrated orally, but that oral drills are unsuitable. Written exercises (of the conversion type) are, in many cases, preferable. The conjunction *as* (introducing a clause expressing reason) is an example. If you ask the question 'Why didn't you come to school yesterday?', the answer would include *because*, but would not normally include *as*. (See § 96.)

As pupils acquire an ever-increasing command of structures and patterns, and as their reading material deals with an ever-widening range of subject matter, it becomes more difficult to provide sequences of statements, requests, and sentences and answers, of the kind that could be provided easily in *Stage One* and *Stage Two*. Oral drills cannot be limited to the classroom environment or to activities that can be carried out in class. This would, in any case, be undesirable. Pupils would find it dull. They must be helped to get outside the classroom.

This raises other problems for the author of a book such as this, which is not designed for one particular country or even one continent. Should teachers, when engaged in the oral presentation of a new item, use contexts and situations confined to their own country, or range freely over the world? This must depend upon local conditions and requirements. A teacher in Italy or Germany, when dealing with *far*, *farther* and *farthest*, will not hesitate to use the names of towns in Europe. A teacher in Indonesia or Nigeria may prefer to use names of places in his own country or continent. There are, in *Stage Three*, many sequences which teachers will take as a guide only. They will follow the procedures that are set out, but will change the contexts, situations and other factors to suit local conditions. There is no point in insisting upon feet, yards and miles, pounds, shillings and pence, gallons and pints, or British place-names and names of British writers, musicians, and so on, if these are likely to be of little use or interest to pupils.

The advice on methods and procedures given in the Introduction to *Stage Two* is not repeated here, but is still useful. The list of phonemes is reprinted, together with the notes on them, and on the tone symbols. It is still important to use the kind of intonation marked in the material in this book. Good models of intonation, and careful imitation of them by the pupil, are always desirable. Good intonation is a greater factor in speech intelligibility than the correct production of vowel and consonant sounds.

The cumulative index printed at the end of this book is of structural words and 'heavy duty' words. There is no index of 'content words' (as in *Stage Two*). This is because pupils are, at this stage, likely to have a large vocabulary of such words. This will vary widely according to the textbooks used. Teachers will know which 'content words' they may safely use in their oral work.

The Tables on pages xv–xlii summarize the material in the sections indicated. They provide a quick reference to the structures here presented.

SOUNDS AND SPELLINGS

PHONEMIC SYMBOLS

1. THE CONSONANTS

Phonemic symbols	Examples			
p	*pen*	pen	*top*	top
b	*bag*	bag	*rub*	rʌb
t	*ten*	ten	*wet*	wet
d	*desk*	desk	*head*	hed
k	*cap*	kap	*back*	bak
g	*get*	get	*bag*	bag
m	*mouth*	mauθ	*come*	kʌm
n	*nose*	nouz	*nine*	nain
ŋ	*sing*	siŋ	*English*	ˈiŋgliʃ
l	*leg*	leg	*well*	wel
f	*face*	feis	*knife*	naif
v	*very*	ˈveri	*five*	faiv
θ	*thin*	θin	*mouth*	mauθ
ð	*these*	ði:z	*mother*	ˈmʌðə*
s	*six*	siks	*face*	feis
z	*nose*	nouz	*his*	hiz
ʃ	*shoe*	ʃu:	*fish*	fiʃ
ʒ	*pleasure*	ˈpleʒə*	*measure*	ˈmeʒə*
r	*right*	rait	*very*	ˈveri
h	*hat*	hat	*head*	hed
tʃ	*chair*	tʃeə*	*teach*	ti:tʃ
dʒ	*jump*	dʒʌmp	*John*	dʒon
w	*window*	ˈwindou	*we*	wi:
j	*yes*	jes	*you*	ju:

2. VOWELS AND DIPHTHONGS

Phonemic symbols	Examples			
iː	*green*	griːn	*three*	θriː
i	*sit*	sit	*this*	ðis
e	*desk*	desk	*leg*	leg
a	*hat*	hat	*back*	bak
aː	*glass*	glaːs	*father*	ˈfaːðə*
o	*box*	boks	*clock*	klok
oː	*ball*	boːl	*draw*	droː
u	*book*	buk	*put*	put
uː	*moon*	muːn	*two*	tuː
ʌ	*sun*	sʌn	*come*	kʌm
əː	*word*	wəːd	*first*	fəːst
ə	*again*	əˈge(i)n	*under*	ˈʌndə*
ei	*day*	dei	*name*	neim
ou	*nose*	nouz	*go*	gou
ai	*five*	faiv	*high*	hai
au	*mouth*	mauθ	*down*	daun
oi	*boy*	boi	*noise*	noiz
iə	*here*	hiə*	*near*	niə*
eə	*chair*	tʃeə*	*where*	weə*
uə	*poor*	puə*	*fewer*	fjuə*

NOTES

1. THE symbols set out in these Tables can be used for a simplified transcription of English. Its advantages are set out in Appendix A of Daniel Jones's *An Outline of English Phonetics* (8th edition, 1956).

Many teachers and students of English are likely to be more familiar with the transcription used in Daniel Jones's *English Pronouncing Dictionary*, in *An Advanced Learner's Dictionary of Current English*, and in numerous textbooks on English phonetics. Others may have become accustomed to the narrow transcription used by I. C. Ward in her *The Phonetics of English* (Heffer, 1929). A table of equivalences for the vowel symbols in the three systems (marked 'Simplified', '*E.P.D.*', and 'Ward') is given below. Consonant symbols are identical in all three systems.

Slant bars / / are used to enclose symbols denoting phonemes and sequences of phonemes when these occur in contexts for which ordinary spelling is used. Slant bars are not used when symbols for phonemes or sequences of phonemes occur in columns (as in the Tables) or when a phonemic transcription is separated clearly from its equivalent in ordinary spelling.

Simplified		*E.P.D.*	Ward
iː	(as in s*ea*t)	iː	i
i	(as in s*i*t)	i	ɪ
e	(as in s*e*t)	e	ɛ
a	(as in s*a*t)	æ	æ
aː	(as in f*a*ther)	ɑː	ɑ
o	(as in h*o*t)	ɔ	ɒ
oː	(as in h*a*ll)	ɔː	ɔ
u	(as in f*u*ll)	u	ʊ

uː	(as in f*oo*l)	uː	u
əː	(as in w*or*d)	əː	ɜ
ei	(as in d*ay*)	ei	eɪ
ou	(as in b*oa*t)	ou	oʊ
ai	(as in b*uy*)	ai	aɪ
au	(as in c*ow*)	au	aʊ
oi	(as in b*oy*)	ɔi	ɔɪ
iə	(as in id*ea*)	iə	eɪ
eə	(as in ch*air*)	ɛə	ɛə
uə	(as in p*oor*)	uə	ʊə

2. Stress is shown, where necessary, by the use of the marks ' and ˌ. The mark ' indicates a primary stress. The mark is placed before the stressed syllable or word: *under* /ˈʌndə/, *again* /əˈge(i)n/. The mark ˌ indicates a secondary stress: *examination* /igˌzamiˈneiʃn/. In this word there is a primary stress on the penultimate syllable and a secondary stress on the second syllable.

The asterisk (as in /weə*/) indicates the possibility of *r*-linking:

Where was it?	weə ˈwoz it?
Where is it?	weər ˈiz it?

The *r*-sound is used when the word that immediately follows begins with a vowel sound.

If a symbol is printed in parenthesis, this indicates an alternative pronunciation. Thus *again*, transcribed as /əˈge(i)n/, indicates that the word may be pronounced either as /əˈgein/ (rhyming with *chain*), or as /əˈgen/ (rhyming with *ten*). The transcription /ˈpous(t)mən/ (for *postman*) indicates that /ˈpoustmən/ may be heard in slow or careful speech and that /ˈpousmən/ is commonly heard at ordinary speed.

The Tone Symbols

Several systems have been devised to indicate pitch level and change of pitch. In this book a very simple system is used.

The symbols used in this book are:

The short horizontal stroke ⁻ to indicate a high-level pitch, and the short horizontal stroke _ to indicate a low-level pitch.

The symbol ⌄ indicates a fall from a high-level pitch to a low-level pitch. The symbol ⌃ indicates a rise from a low-level pitch to a high-level pitch.

Here are examples, with notes.

1. _I'm ⁻touching the ⌄wall.

The words *I'm* are on a low-level pitch. The words *touching the* are on a high-level pitch. There is a fall in pitch on the word *wall*.

2. ⁻Am I touching the ⌃door?

The words *am I* are on a high-level pitch. Because there is a stress on the first syllable of *touching*, the words *touching the* are uttered on a lower pitch. The voice then drops to low-level pitch at the start of the word *door* and rises during the utterance of this word.

Conventional punctuation marks are usually considered adequate in phonemic transcriptions without tone symbols. They are not always adequate, however, in tonetic transcriptions. If, in a statement or question, there is more than one intonation phrase, the boundary may not be indicated by a comma. In the question

⁻Am I touching the ⌃wall or the ⌄door?

the only conventional mark of punctuation is the question mark at the end. There is no mark after *wall* to indicate that with this word one intonation phrase ends.

To indicate tonetic boundaries of this sort a single vertical stroke or bar is used.

ˉAm I touching the ∕wall | or the ∖door?

Other examples of the use of this bar to indicate tonetic boundaries are:

ˉIs this a ∕pen | or a ∖pencil?

The first intonation phrase ends on *pen*.

The ∕green book | is in my ∖right hand. The ∕black book | is in my ∖left hand.

In these two statements attention is called to the adjectives. This is done by the use of a rising tone on *green* and *black* and a falling tone on *right* and *left*. In each statement the first intonation phrase ends on *book*.

Abbreviations
(*Used in Patterns*)

VP	Verb Pattern
S	Subject
v	Finite Verb
V	Non-finite Verb[1]
D.O.	Direct Object
I.O.	Indirect Object
A.P.	Adverbial Particle[2]
(Pro)noun	Noun or Pronoun

[1] i.e. the present and past participles and the infinitive.

[2] i.e. **one** of the short preposition-like adverbs such as *on, off, in, out, up, down, back, away*.

TABLE No. 1

Summary of Material in §§ 1–7

Birmingham		larger / a larger town / more important / a more important town		Leeds.
This problem	is	easier / an easier problem / more difficult / a more difficult problem	than	that one.
This book		more | interesting		that book.
My chair		less | comfortable		your chair.
London		the | largest / most important | town		in Great Britain.
This (chair)		the | most comfortable chair		in the room.

TABLE No. 2

Summary of Material in § 8

This			not so | good / bad	as	that.
My	handwriting	is	better / worse	than	yours.
Tom's					John's.
Which / Whose			the		best? / worst?

TABLE No. 3

Summary of Material in § 9

Bruce Betty	is	older	than	Mark. Jill.
Roger Jill		younger		Mark. Betty.
The	eldest	son	is called	Bruce.
	youngest	boy		Roger.
	elder	daughter		Betty.
	younger	girl		Jill.

TABLE No. 4

Summary of Material in § 10

York	is	farther from	London	than	Leeds.
Oxford					Cambridge.
Which (town)		the farthest from	London:	Oxford, York, or Cambridge?	
Which (country)			this country:	India, Burma, or Thailand?	

TABLE No. 5

Summary of Material in §§ 12–15

He	is	opening closing	the	door window	slowly. quickly.
	walked to				
	spelt			word	correctly. incorrectly.
	wrote				neatly. carefully.

TABLE No. 6

Summary of Material in § 16

John	runs swims jumps plays the piano speaks French	well. badly.		
		better worse	than	Tom. his sister.
		the	best. worst.	

TABLE No. 7

Summary of Material in § 18

Aeroplanes	fly	fast. faster than birds.
John	runs can run	fast. faster than Paul. the fastest.

TABLE No. 8

Summary of Material in § 19

John	pulled pushed	the cart	hard. harder than David.
	works		the hardest.

TABLE No. 9

Summary of Material in § 20

He	usually	gets up goes to bed gets to school	early.
	sometimes	gets up has breakfast	late.

TABLE No. 10

Summary of Material in § 21

Susan read	the letter	aloud. silently. to herself. in a low voice.

TABLE No. 11

Summary of Material in § 22

I like She likes	coffee cheese	very much. a little.
They don't like	jazz climbing mountains	at all.

TABLE No. 12

Summary of Material in § 23

Mary is	much a little a lot	better worse	today.

TABLE No. 13

Summary of Material in §§ 25–26

What is	the house your new teacher the weather	like?
My house is John is (not)	like	yours. his brother.

TABLE No. 14

Summary of Material in § 26

It	is was	hot (cold, warm, cool). raining (snowing, freezing).

TABLE No. 15

Summary of Material in §§ 28–30

These two books are	the same (colour, size). different (colours, sizes).	
My book is	the same as different from	yours.
This flower is	the same colour as a different colour from	that flower.
What is	the difference between	these two boxes ?

TABLE No. 16

Summary of Material in § 32

This is	very much a little not at all	like	that.
	quite different from		

TABLE No. 17

Summary of Material in § 33

It is	easy difficult hard (im)possible	for	him you us Susan	to do that.
	certain likely			to rain. to be hot.

TABLE No. 18

Summary of Material in § 34

Is	English	easy	to learn?
	this word	hard difficult	to spell?
	this water milk	good	to drink?

TABLE No. 19

Summary of Material in §§ 36–37

You know	my name.
	who I am.
	what my name is.
	how to spell my name.
	that my name is Smith.
	where London is.
	that London is the capital of England.

TABLE No. 20

Summary of Material in §§ 38–39

He	says	(that)	he is going to play tennis.
			he has been to the cinema.
			he will help us.
	said told me		he was going to London.
			he came by bus.

TABLE No. 21

Summary of Material in § 41–42

She could	speak English swim run well	when she was five years old.
I couldn't	see the book	when it was in the drawer.

TABLE No. 22

Summary of Material in §§ 45

I	shall				I		my	
You	will	be able	to see well	when	you	get	your	new
They					they		their	glasses.
He	'll				he	gets	his	

TABLE No. 23

Summary of Material in §§ 47–48

You come	to school	to learn things.
Mr. X comes		to give lessons.
He went	to the post-office	to buy some stamps.

I opened the door	for	the cat	to go out.
The bell rang		us	to come to school.

TABLE No. 24

Summary of Material in §§ 49–51

I have	no paper	to write on.
	no pen	to write with.
	nothing	to read.
Have you Is there	anything	to eat? to drink?
It's	time	to start (stop).
What's	the right way	to spell this word?

TABLE No. 25

Summary of Material in § 52

This	word	is	easy	to	spell.
	book		hard		read.
	question		difficult		answer.

TABLE No. 26

Summary of Material in §§ 53–62

The lamp is	on over above	the table.	
My coat is	on over	(the arm of) (the back of)	the chair.
Airliners fly	above	the clouds.	
	over across	the Atlantic.	
Pour the water	over	the floor.	
Write your name	above on below	the line.	
The sun is	above below	the horizon.	
The temperature is	above below	freezing-point.	

TABLE No. 27

Summary of Material in §§ 63–70

If I give Paul this key,	he'll be able to open this box.	
If I drop this glass,	it will break.	
If I gave Paul this key,	he'd be able to he could	open this box.
If I dropped this glass,	it would break.	
If I were rich, I had £10,000	I'd be able to I could	travel round the world.
If you went by air,	it would take only two hours.	

TABLE No. 28

Summary of Material in §§ 71–75

If	we want to buy things,		it is necessary for us to we must		have money.

It is
Is it
Will it be
	necessary	for	you
			them
			him
				to	get up early
					come to school
					  tomorrow
					be here at eight
					  o'clock
					work hard
					answer all these
					  questions

Do you Will they Does he		have			
I don't They don't He doesn't					

TABLE No. 29

Summary of Material in §§ 76–78

He You	must needn't	answer all these questions
Must Needn't	I we	be here at six o'clock

TABLE No. 30

Summary of Material in §§ 79–80

I		need	some new shoes
You			
He		needs	
Do	you they	need	a new hat
Does he			a holiday
I don't			
He doesn't			
We all			to go away for a holiday
You don't			to start yet.

TABLE No. 31

Summary of Material in §§ 81–82

You He	ought to should	go to bed earlier be more careful
Oughtn't Shouldn't	you to you	
You They	oughtn't to shouldn't	eat unripe fruit.

TABLE No. 32

Summary of Material in §§ 83–91

(Illustrating various Tense Sequences)

We	eat	when	we are	hungry.
	drink			thirsty.
	go to bed			tired.
I	wash (myself)	before	I	put my clothes on.
	dress (myself)			have breakfast.
	have breakfast			go to school.
I	put my clothes on	after	I have	washed (myself).
	have breakfast			dressed (myself).
	go to school			had breakfast.
When	I go to X,		I shall see my brother.	
	Tom goes to X,		he will visit the museum.	
	we have finished this Lesson,		we shall start the next Lesson.	
When	he's had his supper,		he will listen to the radio.	
After	I've written the letter,		I shall post it.	
When	we got to the cinema,		the film had already started.	
	he reached the station,		the train had already left.	
We got to the football ground		before	the game had started.	
The bell rang			we had finished our work.	

TABLE No. 33

Summary of Material in § 93

By	now	we	have	read	150	pages.
	last Friday		had		140	
	next Friday		will have		160	

TABLE No. 34

Summary of Material in §§ 95–97

As	she's ill,		she has to stay in bed.
	I had no money,		I couldn't buy the book.
	it was raining,		we didn't go out.
She's ill,			she has to stay in bed.
I had no money,		so	I couldn't buy the book.
It was raining,			we didn't go out.

TABLE No. 35

Summary of Material in § 98

As he was getting off the bus,	he saw Mr. X.
While he was going home,	

TABLE No. 36

Summary of Material in § 99

Although	Mr. X is over 90, he can still see well.
	he went by taxi, he arrived late.

TABLE No. 37

Summary of Material in §§ 101–105

Since	1958,	you've learnt many things.
	you entered this school,	
	you've been here,	

TABLE No. 38

Summary of Material in § 106

Wait	until	the bell rings.
Don't go		I tell you to go.

TABLE No. 39

Summary of Material in §§ 108–115

This box		wood.
The window	is made of	glass.
My shirt		cotton.
Cats		fur.
Birds	are covered with	feathers.
Great Britain		counties.
Japan	is divided into	prefectures.
Switzerland		cantons.
This piece of paper The sleeve of this coat	is torn.	
'Hamlet'		Shakespeare.
This novel	was written by	Dickens.
The boy	was knocked down by a bus. has been taken to hospital.	

TABLE No. 40

Summary of Material in §§ 117–122 (Possibility)

It is	possible probable	that it will	rain	tomorrow.
	It may		be fine	
He may	be ill.			
	have	missed his bus. had a puncture.		
He	may	win	a prize.	
	might	have won		

TABLE No. 41

Summary of Material in §§ 123–125 (Permission)

You may	sit down. go back to your seat.	
May I	ask a question? leave the room?	Yes, you may. No, you may not.
He asked	if whether	he might	open the window. go to the cinema.

TABLE No. 42

Summary of Material in §126 (Prohibitions)

You mustn't	make a noise. leave your bicycle here. leave litter in the park.

TABLE No. 43

Summary of Material in § 129

You'll be	sorry glad	to learn that Susan is	ill. better.

TABLE No. 44

Summary of Material in §§ 130–132

The child was afraid	of the big dog.
	to go near the dog.
Are you ready	for school?
	to start?

TABLE No. 45

Summary of Material in § 133

| I'm | glad | (that) | you're well again. |
| | sorry | | your sister is ill. |

TABLE No. 46

Summary of Material in §§ 137–140

If I	dropped	this glass,	it would	break.	
	had dropped			have broken.	
	asked	you to lift	you could	lift	it.
	had asked	this box,		have lifted	
	went	to	I might	see	the
	had gone	Washington,		have seen	President.

TABLE No. 47

Summary of Material in §§ 144–147

Ask her Do you know	whether		she will be here tomorrow there are any eggs in the house her brother is still in London
Ask him	whether	he came by bus	or whether	he walked here.
		he only reads French		he speaks it, too.

TABLE No. 48

Summary of Material in §§ 150–154

I wish	I		knew French. could go to France. had a map of France.
	you		would help me.
Don't you wish	you	were	rich? a member of the team?
I'm sorry It's a pity	I		don't know French. can't go to France. haven't a map of France.
He	wishes wished	he	had known about it. hadn't made that mistake. could have helped us.

2

TABLE No. 49

Summary of Material in §§ 157–164

This box	is	heavy	I can't lift it.
The ceiling		high	no one can touch it.
The stick		thick	you can't break it.
Susan		ill	she can't come to school.
There are	so	many stars	that	we can't count them.
It costs		much money	I can't buy it.
There was		much rain	the roads were flooded.
		little rain	the crops died.
It was	such	an easy book	that	Tom read it in one hour.
Tom is		a good runner	he wins every race.
I have never met	such	naughty boys	as	Tom, Dick and Harry.
I have never known		clever girls	Mary and Susan.

TABLE No. 50

Summary of Material in §§ 170–173

The book	(that)	I put on Paul's desk	is	green.
The books	(which)	Alan showed me		
		Tom held up	are	
This is	the book	(that)	I borrowed from Tom.	
These are	the books	(which)	Tom lent me.	
Show me	the pen(s)		you bought yesterday.	

TABLE No. 51

Summary o₎ Material in §§ 174–177

The letter	that	came yesterday	is from my brother.
The street	which	goes to the river	is called Bridge Street.
The planes		cross the Atlantic	are usually large.

TABLE No. 52

Summary of Material in § 178

The street	(that)	my brother lives in	is	wide.
The house				small.
The street	in which	my father lives	is	narrow.
The house				large.

TABLE No. 53

Summary of Material in §§ 179–180

The boy	who	cleaned the blackboard	is John.
		has just left the room	
The men		came here last week	were French.

TABLE No. 54

Summary of Material in § 181

The man	(whom)	you met yesterday	was my brother.
The men		you saw	were from India.

TABLE No. 55

Summary of Material in § 182

The man	(that)	I lent my bicycle to	has gone to X.
		I was talking to	is my brother.
The man	to whom	I lent my bicycle	has gone to X.
		I was talking	is my brother.

TABLE No. 56

Summary of Material in § 183

The boy	whose book I borrowed	wants it back.
The man	whose daughter I am going to marry	is very rich.

TABLE No. 57

Summary of Material in §§ 187–190

Write the word			at the top		at the bottom.
Use		either	a pen	or	a pencil.
I shall go there			next week		the week after next.
It's		neither	yellow	nor	brown.
I've visited			Paris		Rome.
Neither	Tom	nor	Harry		is tall. has been to Rome.
	Belgium		Holland		is a large country.
You may have		either neither	of them. of these books.		

TABLE No. 58

Summary of Material in §§ 191–195

	am	I.
	is	he (she, my father, *etc.*).
	are	we (they, Mr. and Mrs. Brown, *etc.*).
So	was	I (he, she, Tom, *etc.*).
	were	you (they, the others, *etc.*).
	have	I (you, they, all of us, *etc.*).
	has	he (she, Harry, *etc.*).
	do	I (you, they, most people, *etc.*).
Neither	does	he (she, Mary, my sister, *etc.*).
(Nor)	did	I (we, you, they, the others, *etc.*).
	shall	I (we).
	will	you (they, he, Miss Jones, *etc.*).
	can	I (we, you, he, they, *etc.*).
	could	I (you, anyone, *etc.*).

TABLE No. 59

Summary of Material in §§ 197–198

Each	boy of the boys	in this class	speaks English well.
He gave	each	girl of the girls	a book.
There is a baker's shop		on each side of	the street.
I have a friend sitting			me.

TABLE No. 60

Summary of Material in § 199

| This book is French, but | every other | book is English. |
| John is absent from school, but | | boy in the class is present. |

TABLE No. 61

Summary of Material in § 200

| Rub out
Write on | every other | line. |
| He goes there | | day (week). |

TABLE No. 62

Summary of Material in § 201

| Some | people like it; | others | don't. |
| | boys work hard; | | are lazy. |

TABLE No. 63

Summary of Material in § 202

| They were | looking at
talking to | each other.
one another. |
| You all know | | |

TABLE No. 64

Summary of Material in §§ 203–204

These	books	are	all both	mine.
	bags	all both	belong to me.	
They	are	both all	working hard. playing football.	
	have		gone to London. read this book.	
	both all	speak English well. like oranges.		

TABLE No. 65

Summary of Material in § 205

What else	is there in the box? did you do? does he want?		
There is	something nothing	else	here in my bag
Is there	anything		

TABLE No. 66

Summary of Material in § 206

Who else	wants to come? can you see? needs help?		
There is	somebody someone nobody no one	else	there in the room outside at the door
Is there	anybody any one		
This is	somebody someone	else's	hat, not mine. book, not yours.

TABLE No. 67

Summary of Material in § 207

Where else		did you go? has he been? can I buy them?	
We shall go	somewhere	else	next year.
	nowhere		today.
Did you go	anywhere		last week?

TABLE No. 68

Summary of Material in §§ 209–211

I	myself	picked up the books.
Mary	herself	went to the door.
You	yourself yourselves	saw what happened.

I	did the work	myself.
She	opened the door	herself.
They	went there	themselves.

TABLE No. 69

Summary of Material in § 212

I saw	Mr Green himself
Did you see	Mrs Green herself
She spoke to	the players themselves

TABLE No. 70

Summary of Material in §§ 213–215

Can Did	you	lift it do the work go there	(all) by	yourself?
	he			himself?
	she			herself ?
	they			themselves?

CHAPTER ONE (§§ 1–10)

COMPARATIVES AND SUPERLATIVES OF ADJECTIVES WITH *MORE* AND *MOST;* IRREGULAR COMPARATIVES

GOOD; BETTER; BEST
BAD; WORSE; WORST
OLD; ELDER; ELDEST
FAR; FARTHER; FARTHEST

§ 1. The three degrees of comparison are usually named Positive, Comparative, and Superlative. It is not necessary for your pupils to learn these names, though they may be given if, in your country, examination requirements include a knowledge of traditional grammatical terminology. Comparatives and superlatives in *-er* and *-est* were dealt with in *Stage Two*.[1] So were the irregular comparatives *many/much, more, most,* and *little, less, least.*[2] Before presenting the new material in this chapter it will be useful to revise quickly this material from *Stage Two*, and also the Comparisons of Equality and Inequality.[2]

§ 2. Adjectives of three or more syllables form the comparative and superlative by the use of *more* and *most*. No firm rules can be given for adjectives of two syllables. Those ending in *-y* usually add *-er/-est* (with *i* for *y*): *early, earlier, earliest; ugly, uglier, ugliest*. So do those ending in *-er*, as *clever, cleverer, cleverest*. Those ending in *-le* add *-r, -st: simple, simpler, simplest*. Those ending in *-ful* take *more* and *most: more/most useful, careful, doubtful*. So do participial adjectives ending in *-ing* and *-ed: more/most learned; more/most charming*. In many cases, however, the choice between *-er/ -est* and *more/most* depends upon such factors as sentence rhythm, and whether or not the two-syllabled adjective is used with a three-

---

[1] See Chapters Twenty-seven and Twenty-nine.

[2] See Chapter Twenty-eight, *Stage Two*.

syllabled adjective (e.g. *the most pleasant and enjoyable* holiday I have ever had instead of *the pleasantest and most enjoyable*). Many two-syllabled adjectives with stress on the first syllable may be compared in either manner: *pleasanter/pleasantest*, or *more/most pleasant; crueller, cruellest*, or *more/most cruel*. Some two-syllabled adjectives with stress on the second syllable may also be compared in either manner: *remoter, remotest* and *more/most remote; profounder, profoundest* and *more/most profound*. Teachers should, therefore, avoid rules, and must be cautious in giving guidance. When examples occur in reading-texts, pupils may be told to observe the ways in which adjectives are compared. They may be told to make a collection (preferably in complete sentences) in their notebooks.

§ 3. *Important* is an adjective likely to be known to your pupils.[1] Start by asking about towns. Here, names of towns in Great Britain are used. You may prefer to use names of towns in your own country.

⌐London, | ⌐Birmingham | and ⌐Leeds | are ⌐towns. They're in ⌐England. ⌐Which is the ⌐largest of these three towns? ⌐London is. It's ⌐larger than ⌐Birmingham. It's ⌐larger than ⌐Leeds.

⌐Which is ⌐larger, | ⌐Birmingham | or ⌐Leeds? ⌐Birmingham is. Birmingham is ⌐larger than ⌐Leeds.

London is an im⌐portant town. It's the ⌐capital of Great ⌐Britain. ⌐Birmingham's an important town, | ⌐too. And ⌐Leeds is an important town. London is the ⌐most important town in Great ⌐Britain. It's a ⌐more important town than ⌐Birmingham. It's a ⌐more important town than ⌐Leeds.

Give repetitions and then put questions to the class. Vary the sequence by using names of other towns in other countries likely to be known to your pupils.

---

[1] If not, give the equivalent in the language of your pupils. Do not waste time here trying to teach new adjectives in other ways.

§ 4. *Difficult* is another adjective likely to be known. Use it with *easy*. If by now your pupils know the English names of their subjects of study, use these words. If not, ask questions about problems in arithmetic (set out on the blackboard). You will know what types of problems are, for your pupils, easy or difficult.

Be careful to avoid structures that have not yet been presented and drilled. Your pupils are probably unfamiliar with the pattern: *It is easy (difficult) to* × infinitive.[1] They may not have learnt the pattern in which a verb (e.g. *know*) is used with a clause introduced by *that*.[2] In the procedures suggested here only those structures, tenses, etc., dealt with in *Stages One* and *Two* are used.

⁻What are your most important ⸜subjects in this school? They're ⸍English, | ⸍science, | ⸍history, | ge⸍ography[3], | a⸍rithmetic, | and ⸜algebra.

⸜Tom, | ⁻is English ⸍easy | or ⸜difficult? (It's ⸜easy, *or* It's ⸜difficult.)

Use *for you* in your next question. Explain this if it is not guessed.

⸜Harry, | ⁻which is ⸜easier for you, | a⸍rithmetic | or ⸜algebra?

⸜Mary, | ⁻which is easier for ⸜you, | ⸍history | or ge⸜ography[3]?

⸜Edith, | ⁻which is more ⸜difficult for you, | ⸍English | or ⸜science?

⁻Which is the ⸜easiest subject for you, Roger? (⸜History is.)

⁻Which is the ⸜most difficult for you, Paul? (⸜Algebra is.)

⁻Which is the most difficult for ⸜you, Alan? (⸜History is.)

⸜Ruth, | ⁻which is ⸜more difficult for you, | ⸍algebra | or ⸜science? (⸜Science is.) (*etc., etc.*)

[1] It is dealt with in Chapter Three below.

[2] It is dealt with in Chapter Four below.

[3] *ge⸍ography* [dʒi'ogrəfi], or *⸍geography* ['dʒogrəfi].

Require pupils to come to the front and put similar questions to their classmates.

§ 5. Here are specimens using problems in arithmetic.[1] Write on the blackboard a series of additions, subtractions, and multiplications, some easy, some difficult, and some rather difficult. E.g. $3 \times 15 = 45$; $11 + 12 = 23$; $16 \div 4 = 4$; $471 \times 9 = ?$; $5621 \div 13 = ?$; $24758 \times 17 = ?$; $58692 \div 1.7 = ?$

It is advisable to have a fairly large number of such problems. If there were only three, one of each class, the question 'Which is the easiest?' would imply that all three were easy. As you ask each question, point to the problem(s).

ˉLook at the ↘blackboard. ˉWhich of these problems are the ↘easiest? ↗These problems are, *or* These on the ↘left are. ˉIs this problem ↗easier | or more ↘difficult than this? It's ↘easier, *or* It's more ↘difficult. ˉWhich is the ↘most difficult? ↗This one is. (*etc., etc.*)

Repeat your questions and require pupils to answer. Ask pupils to come to the blackboard, point to the problems, make statements about them, and put questions to be answered by their classmates.

§ 6. Other adjectives suitable for sequences with *more* and *most* are *beautiful, interesting, famous,* and perhaps *comfortable* and *dangerous.* Whether you use them or not will depend upon the extent of the vocabulary now controlled by your pupils. *Beautiful* can be used with flowers of various kinds (shown, not necessarily named), and perhaps with names of scenic places known to your pupils. *Comfortable* might be used with the noun *seat* (unless the seats in the classroom, including your own, are equally comfortable—or uncomfortable). *Interesting* may be used with subjects of study (as for *difficult*), and perhaps with the name of the subject prefixed to *book.*

ˉWhich is more ↘interesting, | your ↗history textbook | or your ↘science textbook? (*etc., etc.*)

[1] As noted above, you will give problems based on your personal knowledge of what is easy and difficult for your pupils. You may prefer problems in algebra. Do not require pupils to give solutions to the problems. You are teaching English, not mathematics.

Famous is an example of a two-syllabled word used with *more/most*. Make statements about writers, artists and inventors whose names are likely to be known, leading statesmen, *etc*. Ask questions and require answers.

ˉWho's the most famous ˎpoet in this country? ˉWho's the most famous ˎscientist (inˎventor, *etc*.)?

§ 7. When this new material has been mastered, present the use of *less* and *least* with these new adjectives. *Less* was presented in *Stage Two* (see §§ 197–198) in contrast to *fewer*, and *least* (see § 209) in contrast to *fewest*. They are now presented with adjectives.

Here are ˉtwo ˎbooks. This book is ˉless interesting than ˎthis.[1]

Perhaps you can draw simple sketches of three seats: a hard bench, an ordinary chair, and an upholstered armchair.

ˉLook at these three ˎseats. ˉWhich is the most ˎcomfortable? ˎThis one is.[2] ˉWhich is the ˎleast comfortable? ˎThis one is. ˉLook at ˎthis chair, | in the ˎmiddle. Is it ˊmore comfortable | or ˎless comfortable | than the chair on the ˎleft? It's ˎmore (ˎless) comfortable.

It would be tactless to summon girl pupils to the front and make statements with *more/most*, *less/least*, *beautiful*. You may, however, be able to make statements about flowers, pictures on the classroom wall, or scenic places in your country.

§ 8. The irregular comparatives may be presented by using the sequences that follow. They may be used when the words first occur in reading-texts. *Better/best* and *worse/worst* are likely to occur early. *Elder/eldest* and *farther/farthest* are likely to occur much later (if your textbooks are properly graded).

Good, *better*, *best* and *bad*, *worse*, *worst* should not be presented in the same sequences. If you have three drawings they should all be good or all bad. Do not, with only three drawings on display, ask both 'Which is the best?' and 'Which is the worst?' The question 'Which is the best?' implies that all three are good.

[1] Hold up the two books in turn.
[2] Point to your sketches.

Prepare for display three drawings or paintings, all three good, but easily recognizable as 'good', 'better', and 'the best'. Prepare three others which are obviously bad, and recognizable at once as 'bad', 'worse', and 'the worst'. Make statements, ask and answer questions. Add to your statements, if you wish, the names of the objects or articles.

⎺Look at these three ⌄drawings. These are ⌄cats, | ⌄aren't they? These are ⌄good drawings. ⎺Look at the ⌄second drawing. It's ⌄better than the first, | ⌄isn't it? ⎺Look at the ⌄third drawing. It's ⎺better than the ⌄second, | ⌄isn't it? The third is the ⌄best drawing.

As *better* and *best* are irregular your pupils may not see the connexion with *good*. If, after two or three repetitions of the sequence, a request for the equivalent in the mother tongue of *good*, *better*, *best* elicits no correct answer, give an equivalent.

Display, or write on the blackboard, three specimens of good handwriting (using words or sentences which your class will know and understand). Repeat the sequences and this time put questions to the class.

⎺Look at the ⌄blackboard. This handwriting on the left is ⌄good, | ⌄isn't it? ⎺Is this handwriting in the ⌿middle good, | ⌿too? ⌄Yes, | it ⌄is. ⎺Is the handwriting on the ⌿right good, | ⌿too? ⌄Yes, | it ⌄is.

⌄James, | ⎺which is ⌄better, | the ⎺handwriting on the ⌿left | or the handwriting in the ⌄middle? (The handwriting on the ⌄left is better.) ⎺Which is the ⌄best handwriting? (The handwriting on the ⌄right is the best.) (*etc., etc.*)

Using the same displays, or others if your resources allow, call upon pupils to come to the front and make similar statements and put questions to their classmates. Be careful not to choose examples in which *better* and *best* are used as adverbs (e.g. after a verb such as *like*).

Repeat the sequences with displays of bad drawings and bad handwriting to present *bad, worse* and *worst*. Again require pupils to take over from you as soon as their answers to your questions show that they are ready to do so. As often stated in *Stage One* and *Stage Two*, it is important that pupils should have a progressively larger share in this kind of oral work. Pupils are 'ready' to take over when their answers to your questions are fluent and correct. Hesitation and errors are an indication that your own presentation of the new material has been insufficient.

§ **9.** Procedures for *elder/eldest* are simple to devise. Write on the blackboard names of the members of a family (or use a picture prepared in advance, showing the members). Indicate their ages. Here is a specimen:

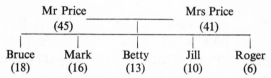

Instead of these English names you may prefer to use names common in your own country. If your pupils have not yet learnt the words *mother, father, brother, sister, son* and *daughter*, they can easily be presented from the diagram (or, more easily, from a picture of the family).

ˉHow many ꜱchildren have Mr and Mrs Price? They have ꜱfive. They have ˉthree sons and two ꜱdaughters. ˉWhat are the ꜱboys' names[1]? (They're ⸍Bruce, | ⸍Mark, | and ꜱRoger). *Or* ˉWhat are the three ꜱboys called[2]? (They're called ⸍Bruce, | ⸍Mark, | and ꜱRoger.) ˉWhat are the two ꜱgirls' names? (They're ⸍Betty | and ꜱJill.) *Or* ˉWhat are the two ꜱgirls called? (They're called ⸍Betty | and ꜱJill.)

ˉHow old is ꜱBruce (ꜱMark, ꜱRoger)? He's ˉeighꜱteen

---

[1] See *Stage One*, § 79.

[2] See *Stage Two*, § 119. (Perhaps you have not yet presented this.)

(ˉsixˎteen, ˎsix). ˉHow old is ˎBetty (ˎJill)? She's ˉthirˎteen (ˎten). ˉHow old is the children's ˎfather? (He's ˉforty-ˎfive.) ˉHow old is their ˎmother? (She's forty-ˎone.)

If the words *son*, *daughter*, *mother* and *father* are new, repeat these sequences until the words are known. If the words *brother* and *sister* are new, present them next.

ˊBruce, | ˊMark, | and ˊRoger | are ˎbrothers. Betty and Jill are ˎsisters. The three boys have ˉtwo ˎsisters. The two girls have ˉthree ˎbrothers.

At this point statements and questions with *older* and *oldest* may be used.

ˉIs Betty ˊolder than Jill | or ˎyounger than Jill? (She's ˎolder than Jill.) ˉWhich of the three boys is the ˎoldest? (ˎBruce is.) ˉWhich of them is the ˎyoungest? (ˎRoger is.) (*etc.*, *etc.*)

This is a revision of material already presented,[1] so not much time should be needed.

The next step is to present *elder* and *eldest*. Whereas *older* and *oldest* may be used of any persons, *elder* and *eldest* are restricted in use to members of the same family[2]. You may explain this to the class in their own language, and then give examples.

Mr and Mrs Price have ˉtwo ˎdaughters. The ˊelder daughter | is (called) ˎBetty. She's ˉthirˎteen. The ˊyounger daughter | is (called) ˎJill. Jill is ˎten. (*Or* She's ˎten.)

Mr and Mrs Price have ˉthree ˎsons. The ˊeldest is | ˎBruce. The ˊyoungest | is ˎRoger.

After repetitions, put questions:

ˉWhat's the ˎelder daughter called? (She's called ˎBetty.)

[1] See *Stage One*, §§ 205, 208.

[2] Special uses (e.g. *the village elders*) do not concern us here.

¯What's the ⌄younger daughter called? (She's called ⌄Jill.)
¯How many ⌄sons are there? (There are ⌄three.) ¯What's
the ⌄eldest son called? (He's called ⌄Bruce.) (*etc.*, *etc.*)

A pupil may then be called out to make statements, and put
questions to his classmates. He may use the same diagram or provide
a new one designed by himself.

§ **10.** The last irregular pair is *farther* and *farthest*. (Do not, at
this stage, refer to *further* and *furthest*.) Start by recalling *far*, *how
far*, *not far* and *a long way*.[1] Then write up on the blackboard names
of a number of places with distances (in miles or kilometres). Here
are specimens with London as the starting point. You may prefer to
use names of places in your own country or your own part of the
world.

Oxford, 55; Cambridge, 50; Leeds, 195; York, 200; Glasgow, 400.

A reproduction on the blackboard of the diagram here will be
easier than a list of names and distances.

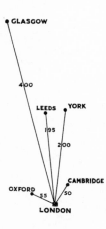

¯Look at these ⌄names. They're
names of places in Great ⌄Britain.
¯How far is it from London to
⌄Oxford, | by ⌄road? It's ¯fifty-five
⌄miles. ¯How far is it from London to
⌄Cambridge by road? It's ⌄fifty miles.
¯Which is ⌄farther from London?
⌄Oxford is farther. It's ¯five ⌄miles
farther.

¯How far is it from London to
⌄Leeds? It's ¯one hundred and ninety-
five ⌄miles. ¯How far is it from London
to ⌄York? It's ¯two hundred ⌄miles.

---

[1] See *Stage Two*, § 166.

⁻Which is ˯farther from London, | ⸍Leeds | or ˯York?
˯York is farther. It's ⁻five miles farther than ˯Leeds.
⁻Glasgow's in ˯Scotland. It's a ⁻long ˯way from London.
It's ⁻four hundred miles by ˯road.

⁻Which of these five places is the ˯farthest from London?
˯Glasgow is.

Repeat sequences of this sort, put questions to the class, and
require pupils to use similar sequences. Instead of towns you may
use names of countries, or places in your district (e.g. names of
public buildings such as the Post-Office, Town Hall, *etc.*).

⁻Which is ˯farther from the school, | the ⸍Post-Office | or
the ˯railway station? (*etc., etc.*)

CHAPTER TWO (§§ 11–23)

ADVERBS OF MANNER AND DEGREE
ADVERBS IN -LY

*WELL, FAST, HARD, EARLY, LATE, ALOUD
(VERY) MUCH; (NOT) AT ALL; A LITTLE;
A LOT*

THE ADJECTIVES *WELL* AND *ILL*

§ **11.** The adverbs and adverbial phrases presented in *Stage One* and *Stage Two* were limited to the adverbial particles (*on, off, up, down, etc.*), adverbials of time (*yesterday, on Sunday, etc.*), adverbials of frequency (*often, never, twice, three times, every day, etc.*), adverbials of duration (*all the morning, for three hours, etc.*), *too* and *enough*, the group *still, already* and *yet*, and adverbial phrases consisting of a preposition and a noun (*on the desk, in my bag, etc.*). Adverbs of manner (answering the question 'How') are now to be presented.

Adverbs formed by the addition of *-ly* to an adjective are presented first. Others, many of them identical in form with adjectives (e.g. *hard, fast, early*), are then presented. Their position in the sentence needs careful treatment.[1]

§ **12.** Adverbs of manner in *-ly* are usually placed after the direct object if there is one and immediately after the verb if there is no direct object. They may have other positions in the sentence, so be careful not to state this as a firm rule. It is useful to have contrasting pairs such as *slowly/quickly, quietly/noisily, softly/loudly, (in)correctly, (im)politely, carefully/carelessly, rightly/wrongly, badly/well.* Your pupils are unlikely to know all of these. Give equivalents in their own language if necessary.

§ **13.** Start with *slowly/quickly*, a pair that is easily demonstrated. As your pupils have learnt the use of *more* and *most* with adjectives,

[1] See *A Guide to Patterns and Usage*, § 104.

you may use the comparative and superlative forms of these adverbs during your presentation of the positive forms.

⁻What am I ˅doing now? I'm ⁻walking to the ˅door. I'm walking ˅slowly. Now I'm ⁻standing at the ˅door. ⁻What am I doing ˅now? I'm ˅opening the door. ⁻How am I ˅opening it? I'm opening it ˅slowly. ˅John,[1] | ⁻come to the ˅door, please. ⁻Walk ˅slowly. ⁻How is John ˅walking? He's walking ˅slowly. I ⁻want you to ˅close the door, John.[2] ⁻Close it ˅slowly, please.

⁻What did I ˅do | two minutes a˅go? I ⁻walked to the door and ˅opened it. ⁻How did I ˅walk? I walked ˅slowly. ⁻How did I ˅open the door? I opened it ˅slowly. ⁻Who ˅closed the door? ˅John did. ˅How did he close it? He closed it ˅slowly.

A further teaching item here is the order in which two or more adverbials are usually placed. Adverbials of direction usually precede adverbs of manner. Adverbials of time usually come last. If, therefore, you combined the statements so far made, the result would be:

⁻What did I ˅do, | ⁻two or three minutes a˅go? I ⁻walked to the door ˅slowly, | a few minutes a˅go.

This order is not fixed, of course. The adverbial of time may come at the beginning for emphasis or contrast, and the adverb of manner may precede the adverbial of direction.

A ⁻few minutes a∕go, | I ⁻walked slowly to the ˅door.

For the present it is better to present your adverbials in the most frequently used order.

§ 14. Repeat the sequences already used, but this time substitute *quickly* for *slowly*. Give more sequences, writing words or sentences

---

[1] Choose a pupil who is a long way from the door.

[2] Do not neglect to revise patterns taught earlier (here, the pattern *v* x (pro)noun x *to*-infinitive).

on the blackboard, first slowly and then quickly. Put questions to the class and require answers. Require pupils to perform activities, make statements about them, and ask questions to be answered by their classmates.

§ **15.** If further sequences are needed, you may ask pupils to write English words on the blackboard and then make statements about the spelling.

ˉHas John spelt the word ↗correctly? ↘Yes, | he ↘has. (*Or* ↘No, | he ↘hasn't.) ˉHas Tom spelt this word ↗correctly | or ↘incorrectly? (*etc., etc.*)

As it is undesirable that pupils should see mis-spellings, choose words that are likely to be spelt correctly. Instead of *spell correctly* you may use *write neatly/carefully/carelessly*.

Further sequences may be given with *quietly/noisily* (e.g. putting books down, closing a window), and *softly/loudly* (e.g. singing, whistling).

§ **16.** *Badly* and *well* should be presented next, and the comparatives *better/worse*, and the superlatives *best/worst*. Link *well* with *good* to help pupils to identify the new adverb.

As it is a sin to discourage young children, avoid telling pupils that they 'speak English badly' or 'spell badly'. You can avoid sinning in this way by doing things badly yourself, for example, drawing blackboard sketches. Then call upon pupils who, you know, have some ability in drawing. Ask them to draw, and then praise their efforts.

ˉLook at these ↘drawings. ˉDo you know what ↗this is?[1] It's a (↘cat). ˉIs it a ↗good drawing? ↘No, | it ↘isn't. It's a ↘bad drawing, | ↘isn't it? I drew this cat very ↘badly, | ↘didn't I? I'm going to draw an↘other cat. ˉIs ↗this a good drawing? ↘No, | it ↘isn't. ↘This drawing is bad, | ↘too. ˉLook at the two ↘cats. They're ˉboth ↘bad drawings, |

[1] See *Stage Two*, § 131. If this pattern for *know* has not yet been presented, do not use this question.

ˋaren't they? The second is ˉworse than the ˋfirst. I drew the second cat ˉworse than the ˋfirst.

Next ask pupils to draw something. While they are busy you may make comments and ask questions.

ˉWhat's ˋTom drawing? He's drawing a ˋtree.[1] ˉIs it a ˊgood drawing? ˋYes, | it ˋis. Tom's drawing ˋwell. ˉWhat's ˋDavid drawing? ˋHe's drawing a tree, | ˋtoo. He's drawing ˋwell. ˉWhat's ˋJohn drawing? ˋHe's drawing a tree, | ˋtoo. ˋHe's drawing well, | ˋtoo.

ˉLook at these three ˋdrawings. ˉWhich is ˋbetter, | ˊTom's tree | or ˋDavid's tree? ˋTom's tree is better. Tom drew ˉbetter than ˋDavid. ˉIs Tom's tree better than ˊJohn's tree? ˋYes, | it ˋis. Tom drew better than ˋJohn. ˉTom drew the ˋbest.

If your pupils have the necessary vocabulary, ask questions about their ability in sports and games. You will probably know the names of the best runners and players in the class (or the school).

ˉDoes Ralph ˊrun (ˊjump, ˊswim) well? (ˋYes, | he ˋdoes.) ˉDoes he run better than ˊyou? ˉWho plays ˋtennis (the) best in this class? Do ˉyou swim better than ˊAlan? ˉCan you swim ˊfarther than Alan?

This type of oral drill has the advantage of getting away from classroom objects and activities and of being of interest to your pupils. It may, however, require the use of many new words and there may not be time for their introduction.

§ 17. There are many adverbs of manner needing individual presentation. Some of them are identical in form with adjectives.[2]

---

[1] You may, of course, put this question to the class instead of answering yourself.

[2] See *A Guide to Patterns and Usage*, § 107 (pp. 194–200).

Examples are *hard, fast, early,* and *late.* It would be wrong to present these together (i.e. to make a 'lesson' from the material). A better plan is to deal with them one or two at a time as they occur in reading-texts. Procedures for presenting them follow.

§ **18.** *Fast* is not a synonym of *quickly. Fast* is linked with speed, whereas *quickly* is linked with time as well as with speed. We may say that an aircraft travels '*faster* than sound', but we say that aircraft enable us to 'get from one place to another quickly', i.e. in a short period of time. In presenting such adverbs, therefore, it is important to do so in suitable contexts. There are some contexts in which *quick* and *fast* are interchangeable. In other contexts they are not inter-changeable. The sequence below uses both *fast* and *quickly,* and shows the difference between them. All the structures have already been presented, but some vocabulary items may need to be given in translation.

⁻If people want to travel ⸝quickly, | they often travel by ⸜air. Aeroplanes are ⸜fast. They're faster than ⸜trains. They're faster than ⸜ships. Aeroplanes ⸜fly fast. They fly faster than ⸜birds, | ⸜don't they?

⁻Which goes ⸜faster, | a ⸝train | or an ⸜aeroplane? An ⸜aeroplane does. ⁻Which goes ⸜faster, | a ⸝train or a ⸜ship? A ⸜train does. ⁻Which goes the ⸜fastest, | a ⸝ship, | a ⸝train, | or an ⸜aeroplane? An ⸜aeroplane goes the fastest.

Repeat the sequence two or three times. Then repeat with questions to the class.

⁻How do people travel if they want to go to (X)[1] ⸜quickly? (They travel by ⸜air.) ⁻Do aeroplanes fly ⸝fast? ⸜Tom, | can ⁻you ⸝run fast? ⁻Can you run faster than ⸝David? ⁻Which can run ⸜faster, | a ⸝horse | or a ⸜cow (an ⸜ox)? (A ⸜horse can.) (*etc., etc.*)

[1] Use the name of a distant place (e.g. London, New York).

When examples occur in reading-texts you may draw attention to the use of *fast* as an adjective, compare the adjective and the adverb, and contrast *fast* and *quick* (e.g. a *quick* journey by a *fast* train).

§ 19. *Hard* is another word that is used both as an adjective and an adverb. Here is a sequence for oral presentation when the word occurs in reading-texts. You may need to give the meanings.

ˌLook, | here's a ˌstick.[1] I'm going to ˉhit the ˌdesk with it. I hit the desk ˌhard.

ˉWhat's ˌthis? It's a piece of ˌrope. ˌTom, | ˉcome ˌhere. ˉTake the end of this ˌrope. ˌPaul, | ˉtake the ˌother end of the rope. ˉNow ˌpull. ˉPull ˌhard. ˉWhich of you is ˌstronger? (ˌPaul is.) (*etc., etc.*)[2]

Further sequences may follow with *push* (e.g. pushing a heavy piece of furniture). Put questions to pupils about the activities.

ˉWhat did I ask (tell) Paul to ˌdo?[3] (You asked him to ˉpull (ˉpush) the ˌtable.) ˉDid I ask him to pull it ⁄hard? (ˌYes, | you ˌdid.) ˉHow did you pull the ˌtable, Paul? (I pulled it ˌhard.)

Work hard will provide further examples. With *work* you may present a new use of *at;* to work hard *at* English (history, geography, *etc.*).

§ 20. *Early* and *late* are useful words. They provide the opportunity of presenting *get* in one of its commonest meanings (arrive).

I came to school this morning at (a ˉquarter to ˌeight).[4] I got to school ˌearly. I ˌalways get to school early. I ˉnever get to school ˌlate. ˌSusan, | ˉdo ⁄you always get to school

---

[1] This pattern for *here* is dealt with in *Stage One*, § 137. Revise if necessary.
[2] If not too much disturbance is likely, you can have a tug-of-war for further examples of *pull hard*(*er*).
[3] See *Stage Two*, §§ 88–89.
[4] Give whatever time is appropriate for an early arrival.

early? (ˏYes, | I ˏdo, *or* ˏNo, | I ˏdon't.) Do ˊyou ever get to school late, Joan? (*etc., etc.*)

To illustrate these words as adjectives you may talk about breakfast.

I usually have breakfast at ⁻seven o'ˏclock. Sometimes I have an ˏearly breakfast. Sometimes I have my breakfast ˏearly. I have it at ⁻half past ˏsix. On ˊSundays¹ | I often have a ˏlate breakfast. I have my breakfast ˏlate.

Use any other sequences that are practicable (for situations, vocabulary, *etc.*) and put questions to the class. *Get up* and *go to bed* are suitable for use with *early* and *late*. Require pupils to make statements and ask questions.

§ **21.** *Aloud* is another adverb of manner that is worth presenting for classroom use. The difference between *aloud* and *loudly* will need explanation. You may also present the adverbs *silently* and *quietly.*

ˏLook, | this is a ˏbook. I'm going to ˏread.² ⁻What have I been ˏdoing? I've been ˏreading.³

I'm going to read aˏgain.⁴ ⁻What have I been ˏdoing? I've been ˏreading again. This time I read aˏloud. The ˊfirst time | I read ˏsilently. The ˊsecond time | I read aˏloud.

ˏMary, | ⁻open your book at page ˏtwelve. I want you to read the ⁻first ˏsentence. ⁻Read it aˏloud. ⁻How did Mary read that ˏsentence? She read it aˏloud. ⁻Now read the ˏsecond sentence. ⁻Read it ˏsilently. ⁻How did you read ˏthat sentence, Mary? (I read it ˏsilently.)

¹ Or Fridays (if you are in a Muslim country where Friday is the holiday).

² Now read for a few seconds silently.

³ The Present Perfect Continuous was presented in § 214 of *Stage Two.* You may need to recall it.

⁴ Now read two or three sentences aloud to the class.

This sequence may be used for presenting and drilling such phrases as *in a whisper*, *to yourself* (i.e. silently), *in a low voice*. These need not be presented until they occur in reading-texts or are found useful in classroom work.

Repeat these and similar sequences and put questions. Require pupils to use similar sequences.

§ **22.** Three adverbs of degree were presented in *Stage Two*. They are *very*, *too* and *enough* used with adjectives.[1] The use of *much*, *not at all*, and *a little* is likely to occur in third-year work. They will probably occur with the verb *like* in reading material.

Much, adverb of degree, normally has end-position. It may precede an infinitive, as in 'I don't much like the plan', but does not come between a verb and its object. Your pupils must be helped to see the difference between *much* used with nouns for quantity,[2] and *much* used with verbs for degree. They must see the difference in meaning between 'Tom likes ice-cream very much' and 'Tom likes very much ice-cream'.[3]

Start with *like* followed by nouns. Later present *like* with verbal nouns (or gerunds).[4] Do not, at present, give examples of *like* with *to*-infinitives. (These are better postponed until *would/should like to* is presented.) Give the meaning of *like* in the language of your pupils. Make statements about your own likes and dislikes, adding *very much*, *(not) at all*, and *a little*.

I like ˅coffee (˅tea, Coca-˅cola, ˅oranges, ˅mangoes, *etc.*). I ‾don't like ˅milk (˅beer, ˅cheese, *etc.*).

I like coffee ‾very ˅much. I like ˅oranges very much, | ˅too. I don't like cheese at ˅all.

I like ˅swimming. I like ˅travelling.

I like swimming ‾very ˅much. I like ˅travelling very much. I ‾don't like climbing mountains at ˅all.

[1] See *Stage Two*, §§ 81–85.

[2] See *Stage Two*, §§ 62–69.

[3] This is grammatically correct, but it is more idiomatic to say 'Tom likes *a lot of* ice-cream'.

[4] This is VP17 in *A Guide to Patterns and Usage*.

The vocabulary you use here will be drawn from that used in the reading-texts. If enough suitable words are not yet known do not hesitate to use others (giving the equivalents in the language of your pupils). If these words are not remembered, do not worry. They are being used only incidentally, as you present the pattern for *like* and the use of adverbs of degree.

Next ask and answer questions.

ˉDo I like ˊcoffee? ˋYes, | I ˋdo. I like it ˉvery ˋmuch.
ˉDo I like ˊcheese? ˋNo, | I ˉdon't like cheese at ˋall.
ˉDo I like ˊswimming? ˋYes, | I ˋdo. I like it ˉvery ˋmuch.

Next put questions to the class.

Do ˉyou like ˊoranges, John? (ˋYes, | I ˋdo, *or* ˋYes, | I like them ˉvery ˋmuch.) ˉDo you like going to the ˊmountains, David? ˉDo you like ˊclimbing mountains?

You may also use names of authors and books likely to be known to your pupils, and perhaps ask whether they like music (European music, Chinese music, jazz, possibly names of instruments).

ˉDo you like piˊano music, Mary? ˉDo you like ˊjazz, Edith? (ˋYes, | I like it very ˋmuch, *or* ˋNo, | I ˉdon't like it at ˋall, *or* ˋYes, | I like it a ˋlittle.)

§ **23.** The adverb *well* is presented in § 16 above. *Well* is also an adjective, used predicatively and contrasted with *ill*. When this adjective occurs in oral work or reading-texts you will have opportunities for using *much*, and *a little* with the comparatives *better* and *worse*. You may do so, in a real situation, if one of your pupils is absent through illness.

Susan isn't at ˋschool today. She's not ˋwell. She's ˋill. She isn't ˋvery ill. She'll be ˉback at school ˋsoon.

A day or two later:

Susan ˉisn't back at school ˋyet. But she's ˉmuch ˋbetter (*or* a ˉlot ˋbetter, a ˉlittle ˋbetter) today.

This type of presentation, made incidentally as occasion offers, is often possible and usually valuable. It has the advantage of giving pupils confidence in their increasing ability to understand and use English for ordinary happenings and affairs. They are taking a school subject outside the classroom.

THIS (BOOK) IS LIKE THAT (BOOK)
WHAT IS IT (THE WEATHER) LIKE?
IT IS HOT (COLD); IT IS RAINING
THE SAME (AS); DIFFERENT (FROM)
THE DIFFERENCE BETWEEN
THIS IS VERY MUCH
(A LITTLE, NOT AT ALL) LIKE . . .
IT IS EASY (HARD) TO × INFINITIVE
IT IS POSSIBLE (FOR YOU)
TO × INFINITIVE
(THIS SUBJECT IS) *EASY (HARD)*
TO LEARN
THIS IS GOOD (BAD) TO EAT (DRINK)

§ **24.** In this chapter some new uses of *it* are dealt with. Your pupils know *it* as a pronoun in such sequences as:

This is a book. It is red.

Take this pen. Give it to John.

They have also used *it* with *a long way*, *not far*, *half a mile*, *ten minutes' walk*, *etc.*[1] They will now learn to use *it* in such statements as 'It is hot', 'It is raining', and its use to anticipate a deferred subject, as in '*It* is easy *to do that*'.

§ **25.** For presenting the use of *it* in such statements as 'It is hot', a useful starting-point is the adjective *like* and the question 'What is . . . like?' Your pupils may know the nouns *sort* and *kind*.[2] If so, this is also a useful starting-point.

[1] See *Stage Two*, § 166.

[2] See *Stage Two*, § 12.

‾What kind of ⸜pencil is this?[1] It's a ‾long ⸜yellow pencil. ‾What kind of pencil is ⸜this?[2] ⸜This is a long yellow pencil, | ⸜too. ⸝This pencil | is like ⸜this pencil.[3]

Repeat with other pairs of identical objects, for example, two large red books, two small white flowers, two long pieces of white chalk.
After these repetitions, ask and answer questions.

‾Look at this ⸜flower. ‾Is it like ⸝this one? ⸜Yes, | it ⸜is. ‾Look at this piece of ⸜chalk. ‾Is it like ⸝this one? ⸜Yes, | it ⸜is.

Repeat your questions and require answers, sometimes long and sometimes short.

‾Is the pencil in my right hand like the pencil in my ⸝left hand? ⸜Short answer, Tom. (⸜Yes, | it ⸜is.) ‾Is the flower in my left hand like the flower in my ⸝right hand? ⸜Long answer, David. (⸜Yes, | the flower in your ⸝left hand | is ‾like the flower in your ⸜right hand.) (*etc., etc.*)

Next present *what . . . like*.

‾Look at ⸜this flower. ‾What's it ⸜like? It's ⸜small. It's ⸜white. ‾Look at ⸜this flower. ‾What's ⸜this flower like? It's ⸜large. It's ⸜red. ‾Look at this ⸜book. ‾What's it ⸜like? It's ⸜thick. It's ⸜brown. It's a ‾thick ⸜brown book.[4] ‾What's ⸜this book like? It's ⸜heavy. It's ⸜black. It's a ‾heavy ⸜black book.[4]

Put these and similar questions to the class. Require pupils to come forward (or stand up at their desks) and make similar statements and ask similar questions.

[1] Hold up the pencil in your right hand.
[2] Hold up an identical pencil in your left hand.
[3] Hold up the two pencils in turn.
[4] Note that the adjectives indicating colour come second.

§ 26. Next ask questions about the weather. You will probably need to give your pupils the meaning of the question, and of the words you use in your answers. Your chief concern here is the new use of *it:* it will be uneconomical of time to try to teach such words as *weather* and *raining* entirely through English.

⁻What's the ↘weather like today? It's ↘hot (↘warm, ↘cold, ↘cool). *Or* It's ↘raining (↘snowing).

These questions and answers do not fit into drills. You should ask such questions from time to time (at the beginning of a lesson, with questions about the day of the week and the date) until pupils answer without hesitation.

§ 27. With the adjective *like* it is convenient to present *same* and *different*. There is the opportunity of recalling and practising the verbs *ask* and *tell* in patterns that are (probably) familiar.[1] There is the opportunity of practising adverbials of degree, as presented in the preceding chapter. When a teaching item has been presented, it should, whenever possible, be recalled and used regularly.

§ 28. For the procedures below a number of objects that are similar or identical are needed, with others of the same kind but different in some way. Hold up two objects that are the same in some way.

⁻Look at these two ↘flowers. ⁻Both these flowers are ↘red, | ↘aren't they? These two flowers are the ⁻same ↘colour. They're ⁻both ↘red.[2]

⁻Look at these two ↘books. ⁻Both these books are ↘brown, | ↘aren't they? These two books are the ⁻same ↘colour. They're ⁻both ↘brown.

⁻Look at ↘these two flowers. ⁻Are ↗these flowers the same colour? ↘No, | they're ↘not. *Or* ↘No, | they ↘aren't. One of them is ↗red; | the other's ↘yellow. These two flowers are ↘different colours.

[1] See *Stage Two*, §§ 93–94.
[2] For these uses of *both*, see *Stage One*, §§ 155–156.

Give more sequences and put questions to the class. Then present *the same . . . as*, *different from*, and *the difference between*. Start by talking about books that are identical, for example, the English textbook used in your class.

˥Hold up your ˎbook, David. ˥What ˎcolour is it? (It's ˎgreen.) ˥Hold up ˎyour book, Paul. ˥Are the two books the same ˊcolour, John? (ˎYes, | they ˎare.) Paul's book is the ˥same colour as ˎDavid's. ˎTom, | ˥hold up ˎyour book. ˥Is your book the same colour as ˊDavid's? (ˎYes, | it ˎis.) (*etc., etc.*)

After similar sequences (using flowers, pens, and whatever else is suitable and available), require pupils to make statements and put questions to their classmates.

§ **29.** Now show a book of your own, clearly not the same as the textbooks recently shown.

˥Look at ˎthis book. ˥Is it the same colour as ˊDavid's, | and ˊPaul's, | and ˊTom's? ˎNo, | it ˎisn't. It's a ˎdifferent colour. It's ˎblue. My book is ˎdifferent from those.

Use other objects, for example, articles of clothing.

˥Look at my ˎhat. ˥Is it the same as ˊyour hat, David? (ˎNo, | it ˎisn't.) My hat's ˎdifferent from yours. Our hats are ˥not the ˎsame, | ˎare they? My hat's ˎlarger than yours, David. It's a different ˎsize (ˎshape, ˎcolour).

Require pupils to make similar statements and ask similar questions.

§ **30.** Next present *the difference between*. Use lines on the blackboard.

˥Look at these two ˎlines. Are they the ˊsame | or are they ˎdifferent? They're ˎdifferent, | ˎaren't they? One's

ˌ⌐long; | the other's ↘short. One's ↗white; | the other's ↘blue.

⌐What's the ↘difference between these two lines? One's ↗long | and ↗white; | the other's ↘short | and ↘red. *Or,* One's long and ↗white; | the other's short and ↘red.[1]

Continue with other contrasted pairs. Use vocabulary items already taught, especially pairs that need to be recalled and practised (e.g. *full/empty, heavy/light, tall/short*).

⌐Look at these two ↘boxes. ⌐Are they the ↗same | or ↘different? They're ↘different. This box is ↘small. It's ↘light. It's ↘empty. This box is ↘large. It's ↘heavy. It's full of ↘sand. ⌐What's the ↘difference between these two boxes? One is ↗small, | ↗light, | and ↘empty; | the other's ↘large, | ↘heavy, | and full of ↘sand.

After the usual drills, give your pupils model sentences on the blackboard to be copied into their notebooks, so that they have a record of the new patterns: *the same* × adj. × *as; different from; the difference between.* New words and phrases of this kind must always be learnt in sentences, not in isolation, especially when prepositions enter into them.

§ 31. Next present the new material with *tell* and *ask*.

⌐What's this ↘box like? It's ↗small, | ↗light, | and ↘empty. I've ⌐told you what this box is ↘like. ⌐What's ↘this box like? It's ↗large, | ↗heavy, | and full of ↘sand. ↘Tom, | ⌐take this ↘box. ⌐Ask Harry what it's ↘like. (⌐What's this box ↘like, Harry? It's ↗small, | ↗light, | and ↘empty.) ⌐What did Tom ↘ask Harry? He asked him

---

[1] The difference between the last two sentences is that in the first you make a pause after *long* and *short* (uttered with a change in pitch); in the second there is no pause after *long* and *short*.

ˉwhat the box is ↓like. ˉWhat did Harry ↘tell Tom? He
told him ˉwhat the box is ↓like. (*etc., etc.*)

§ **32.** Next use *like* with adverbials of degree: *very much, not at all*,
and *a little*. *A little* may be postponed until its adverbial use occurs in
reading material.

If you have brothers or sisters in your class who are alike, this will
be a help. If not there may be pupils who resemble one another. You
may talk about the weather in your country at different times of the
year, or perhaps the scenery in different parts of the country. These
questions must depend to some extent upon the vocabulary with
which, by now, your pupils are familiar from their reading. The
specimens that follow should, therefore, be taken only as a guide to
procedures. It will probably be wise to present this new material
some weeks after the presentation of adverbials of degree with the
verb *like* (as in § 22 of this book). This postponement will lessen the
likelihood of confusion between 'She likes milk very much (a little)'
and 'A is very much (a little) like B.'

ˉWhat's the ↘weather like today? It's ↘hot (↘cold, ↘dry,
etc.). ˉIs the weather now like the weather in ↗May?[1]
↘No, | it's not at ↘all like the weather in May. *Or* ↘Yes, |
the weather now is ˉvery much like the weather in ↓May.

If your pupils know the word *climate* (and can distinguish it from
weather), you may ask questions such as these:

ˉIs the climate of our country like the climate of
(↗England)?[2] ↘Yes, | it ↘is. *Or* ↘No, | the climate of our
country is ˉnot at ↘all like the climate of (England). ˉIs
our climate like the climate of (↗Burma)? ↘Yes, | it's ˉvery
much like the climate of (↓Burma).

---

[1] Choose your months according to the climate in your country.

[2] Do not use *that* (for *the climate*) here unless your pupils are already
familiar with this use of *that*.

Questions about animals may be used if the names are known (e.g. from reading Aesop's Fables), or if wall pictures are available. The adverb *quite* (meaning 'completely') may be used.[1]

⁻Is a rabbit like a ↗hare? ↘Yes, | it ↘is. It's a ↘little like a hare. ⁻Is a rabbit like a ↗tortoise? ↘No, | a rabbit is ⁻not at ↘all like a tortoise. It's ⁻quite ↘different. ⁻Are donkeys like ↗horses? ↘Yes, | they're a ↘little like horses, | but horses are ↘larger. ⁻Are horses like ↗camels? ↘No, | they're not at ↘all like camels. They're ⁻quite ↘different.

When pupils have heard repetitions of these and similar sequences, so that they recognize the word order used in them (adverbials preceding *like*), put questions to be answered by the class. Require pupils to make statements and ask questions.

§ 33. *It* is used to anticipate a deferred subject, as in '*It is easy to do that*'. To present this use of *it* you may start by recalling the verb *can*.[2] The words *easy* and *difficult* are probably known.

⁻Come ↘here, Mary. ⁻Can you lift this ↗chair? (↘Yes, | I ↘can.) ⁻Can you lift this ↗table (↗book-case)? (↘No, | I ↘can't.) ⁻Lift the ↘chair, Mary. It's ↘easy to lift the chair. ⁻Try to lift the ↘table again. You ↘can't. It's ↘difficult to lift the table. It's too ↘heavy. The table's ⁻too ↘heavy for you to lift.[3] You're not ↘strong enough to lift it.

⁻Come ↘here, Susan.[4] ⁻Can you touch the middle of the ↗blackboard? (↘Yes, | I ↘can.) It's ↘easy to touch the middle of the blackboard, | ↘isn't it? ⁻Can you touch the

---

[1] *Quite* is a difficult adverb, used in many ways. If you use it, be careful to do so only in the meaning suggested here, 'completely'.

[2] See *Stage Two*, Chapter Seven.

[3] Here you are recalling and revising the material in *Stage Two*, Chapter Twelve.

[4] Call upon a pupil who is not quite tall enough to touch the top of the blackboard.

ꜛtop of the blackboard? (ꜜNo, | I ꜜcan't.) It's ꜜdifficult
for you to touch the top of the blackboard, | ꜜisn't it?

Note that you have used *for you* in the last statement. This use of
for you should not be a difficulty; it has already been presented with
too and *enough*.

Repeat with other sequences and other adjectives. *Possible* and
impossible are useful words. They enable you to recall such phrases as
by road (*sea, air*).

⁻Can we go from here[1] to London by ꜛair? (ꜜYes, | we
ꜜcan.) It's ⁻possible to go from here to London by ꜜair.
⁻Is it possible to go from here to London by ꜛroad?
ꜜNo, | it ꜜisn't. It's imꜜpossible to go from here to London
by road. ⁻Is it possible to travel to the ꜛmoon yet? (ꜜNo, |
it's imꜜpossible to travel to the moon yet.)[2]

When you put questions to the class you may ask about the
subjects they study, their everyday life, *etc*. Include questions with *or*.

Is it ꜛeasy | or ꜜdifficult for you | to learn ꜜEnglish
(ꜜscience, *etc*.)? Is it ꜛeasy | or ꜜdifficult for you | to get up
ꜜearly (to get to ꜜschool early)?

Certain and *likely* are used in this pattern, so you may give examples
when these words occur in reading material. *Weather* and *climate* are
suitable for examples.

⁻Is it likely to ꜛrain this afternoon? ꜜYes, | it ꜜis. *Or*,
ꜜNo, | it ꜜisn't likely to rain this afternoon.

⁻Which are the ꜜhottest (ꜜcoldest) months of the year in
our country? (They're ꜜ . . . .) ⁻Is it ꜛcertain to be hot
in . . . ? (ꜜYes, | it ꜜis. It's ꜜcertain to be hot in . . . .)

[1] Or the name of a town in your country from which there are regular
flights to London.

[2] If, by the time you deal with this material, cosmonauts have reached
the moon, accept the answer 'Yes', and then put a question using the
name of one of the planets (e.g. Mars or Venus).

Care is needed in the choice of adjectives. We may say 'It is certain (likely) to be hot' but 'probable to be hot' is not English. Do not give your pupils lists of adjectives for use in various patterns. It is better to require your pupils to collect examples (preferably indexed) in their notebooks.

§ **34.** When this use of *it* to anticipate an infinitive phrase has been mastered, you may present the use of adjectives followed by a *to*-infinitive. This need not be dealt with until examples occur in reading material. Specimen procedures follow. *Hard* (= difficult) may be used.

⁻Is English ⸝easy | or ⸜difficult to learn? Is a⸝rithmetic easy to learn | or ⸜hard to learn? ⁻Are my questions ⸝easy to answer | or ⸜hard to answer? Is your textbook ⸝easy to read | or ⸜hard to read? ⁻Are all English words ⸝easy to spell | or are some of them ⸜hard to spell?

⁻Are apples (oranges, *etc.*) good to ⸝eat? ⸜Yes, | they ⸜are. ⁻Is milk good to ⸝drink? Is ⸝ink good to drink? Is ⁻dirty ⸝water good to drink? Is ⸝clean water good to drink?

Restrict the adjectives you use in this pattern to *easy, difficult, hard, good* and *bad*. There are many adjectives that cannot be used in this pattern. We do not say 'This door is possible to open' or 'That question is possible to answer'. Although the sentence 'These questions are impossible to answer' might be used in some contexts, it is preferable, at this stage, to give your pupils the sentence 'It is impossible to answer these questions'.

NEW PATTERNS FOR *KNOW, SAY, TELL*

§ 35. The verb *know* was presented in *Stage Two*.[1] It was used with nouns, as in 'I know your name', and with dependent questions introduced by *what*, as in 'You know what there is in this box'. The verb *say* was also presented in *Stage Two*,[2] but only with simple greetings and formulas as 'Good morning' and 'Thank you'. *Tell* was presented in *Stage Two* in three patterns: *tell* × (pro)noun × *to*-infinitive; *tell* × I.O. × D.O.; *tell* × (pro)noun × dependent question.[3]

Four new verb patterns are now to be presented: *know* followed by a clause introduced by an interrogative adverb or pronoun, *know* followed by an interrogative adverb and an infinitive, *know* and *say* × *that*-clause, and *tell* × (pro)noun × *that*-clause.

§ 36. Start with *know* and recall the patterns with which your pupils are already familiar.[4] Then present the new pattern in which a dependent question follows the verb. Tell one of your pupils to come to the blackboard.

⁻Who's this girl at the ˅blackboard? ⁻Do you know her ∕name? ˅Yes, | you ⁻all know her ˅name. Her name is ˅Susan. ⁻What's ˅my name? You ⁻all know what ˅my name is, | ˅don't you? It's (˅X).[5]

Next ask a series of questions, and, after they have been answered, make statements with *know* (VP 14 and VP 13).

---

[1] See §§ 129–133.

[2] See §§ 177–182.

[3] See §§ 89–94. These are VP 3, 19 and 16 in *A Guide to Patterns and Usage*.

[4] These are VP 15, 13, 11 and 12 in *A Guide to Patterns and Usage*.

[5] Note that it is usual in English not to use any prefix. It is usual to say 'My name is Smith' (not 'Mr Smith' or 'Professor Smith').

‾Where's the ⌄chalk, Susan? (It's in that ⌄box.) Susan ‾knows where the ⌄chalk is. ‾Do you know the word ⸌holiday, Susan?[1] (⌄Yes, | I ⌄do.) ‾Do you know how to ⸌spell this word, Susan? (⌄Yes, | I ⌄do.) Susan ‾knows how to spell ⌄holiday. ‾Write it on the ⌄blackboard, please. Is that ⸌right | or ⌄wrong, Mary? (It's ⌄right.) ‾How many letters are there in the word ⌄school, Susan? (There are ⌄six.) Susan ‾knows how many letters there are in the word ⌄school.

Call upon other pupils to answer simple questions beginning with interrogative adverbs or pronouns. After each answer make statements with *know*.

‾Who's the best ⌄runner in this school, Tom? (⌄X is.) Tom ‾knows who the best ⌄runner in this school is. ‾When do the summer ⌄holidays start, Paul? (They start on the ‾third of ⌄June.) Paul ‾knows when the summer ⌄holidays start. (*Or* Paul ‾doesn't ⌄know when the summer holidays start.)

There are scores of questions of this kind that you may ask. Choose them so that the vocabulary items needed are known by your pupils. When pupils have heard numerous examples of statements with *know*, require some of them to ask questions and then make statements. If, in their statements, pupils fail to convert the question form to the affirmative form (if, for example, a pupil says 'He knows how many letters are there in the word *school*') you must give further examples yourself, and perhaps point out the change in word order.

§ 37. In a later lesson period present *know* with *that*-clauses. Again start with a familiar pattern.

‾Who's the boy near the ⌄door? ‾Do you know his ⸌name? ‾Do you know who he ⸌is? (⌄Yes, | I ⌄do. His name's ⌄Paul, *or* He's ⌄Paul.) ⌄Yes, | his name's ⌄Paul.

[1] Choose a word whose spelling is certainly known.

You ⁻all know his ↓name. You ⁻all know that his name is ↓Paul.

This is, if you have followed the order in which teaching items are arranged in these books, your first use of *that* as a conjunction. You should use the weak form /ðət/; the strong form /ðat/ is rarely used.

Give further sequences[1] and then require pupils to ask similar questions and make statements using the conjunction *that* after *know*.

I have ⁻something in this ↓box. You can't ↓see it. You ⁻don't ↓know what I have (*or* what there is) in this box. It's a ↓ball. Now you ↓know what I have in this box. You know that there's a ↓ball in this box.

Note the weak forms in this last sentence.
ju nou ðət ðəzə ↓bɔːl in ðis boks.

⁻Where's ↓London? (It's in ↓England.) You ⁻all know where ↓London is. You ⁻all know that it's in ↓England. ⁻Do you know where ↗Glasgow is, Paul? (It's in ↓Scotland.) ↓Yes, | it's in ↓Scotland. You ⁻know where ↓Glasgow is. You ⁻know (that) it's in ↓Scotland.

At this point, when pupils have heard very many examples of the conjunction *that*, you may tell them that it is often omitted.

If further examples are needed you may make a series of statements such as these. You may ask pupils to repeat them, using *we* instead of *you* and carefully following your stress and intonation.

You ⁻all know that two and two are ↓four. You ⁻all know that the capital of Italy is ↓Rome. You ⁻all know that today is ↓Monday. You ⁻all know the ↓date, | ↓don't

---

[1] See *Stage Two*, §§ 130–131 for suggestions.

you? ‾What ⌄is the date today, Mary?[1] (It's the ‾first of
⌄May.)

§ 38. Next present *say* in this new pattern. The presentation of
say should be made so that there are no difficult problems caused by
sequences of tenses. There will be changes of pronouns, and it is
better not to have more difficulties than necessary. See that there is
no change of tense necessary. You may do this by using statements
only about what continues to be true.

‾What day of the ⌄week is it, Paul? (It's ⌄Tuesday.)
Paul says that it's ⌄Tuesday. Is ‾that ⁄right, David?
(⌄Yes, | it ⌄is.) ‾What's the ⌄date, John? (It's the ‾first of
⌄May.) John says (that) it's the ‾first of ⌄May. Is ‾that
⁄right, Alan? (⌄Yes, | it ⌄is.) ‾What ⌄year is it, Alan?
(It's ‾nineteen sixty-⌄two.) Alan says (that) it's ‾nineteen
sixty-⌄two. Is ‾that ⁄right, Roger? (⌄Yes, | it ⌄is.) ‾What's
the longest river in ⌄Africa, Harry? (It's the ⌄Nile.) Harry
says (that) the ‾longest river in Africa is the ⌄Nile. (*etc.*,
etc.)

Give further examples. If you ask questions on general knowledge
(like the question about the Nile), be careful to ask only for facts
which your pupils are certain to know. You are giving an English
lesson, not a test on other subjects.

Require pupils to ask similar questions of their classmates and,
after each answer, make a statement with *says* (*that*). If your pupils
are now able to talk about their out-of-class activities, you may ask
questions about these.

‾What are you going to do on ⌄Sunday, Colin? (I'm
going to play ⌄tennis.) Colin says he's going to play
⌄tennis on Sunday. ‾What are ⌄you going to do, Tom?
(⌄I'm going to play tennis, | ⌄too.) Tom says ⌄he's going
to play tennis, | ⌄too.

[1] Note the fall in pitch on *is* in this question.

When pupils use *say* in this pattern confidently and correctly, you may present examples of *said* followed by a past tense form. A suitable procedure is a series of activities with *going to*.

I'm going to sit ˎdown. Now I'm going to stand ˎup. ˉWhat did I ˎsay, | a few moments aˎgo ? I said I was going to sit ˎdown. Then I said I was going to stand ˎup.

This sequence requires changes in tense but not in the pronouns, so you are again keeping changes to a minimum. You may next require pupils to do things.

I ˉwant you to walk to the ˎdoor, Paul. ˉWhat are you going to ˎdo ? (I'm going to ˉwalk to the ˎdoor.)

When Paul has reached the door, continue :

ˉWhat did Paul say he was going to ˎdo ? He said (that) he was going to ˉwalk to the ˎdoor.

You may then continue by telling Paul to open the door, close it, and walk back to his seat. You may put the questions to members of the class instead of answering them yourself.

Use *will* and the Present Perfect in questions for variety.

This month is ˎMay. ˉWhat will ˎnext month be, Mary ? (It will be ˎJune.) Mary says that next month will be ˎJune.

ˉHave you been to the ˏcinema this week, Joan ? (ˎYes, | I ˎhave, *or* ˎNo, | I ˎhaven't.) Joan says she has (*or* she's) been to the ˎcinema this week, *or* Joan says she ˉhasn't been to the ˎcinema this week.

The more involved problems that arise with *say* in reported speech may be dealt with later, when the textbook (or your Syllabus) makes it necessary to deal with them.

§ 39. The last of the three verb patterns presented in this chapter is that in which a verb is followed by a noun or pronoun and then by a clause introduced by *that*. *Tell* is the most important verb used in this pattern. Others are *remind*, *inform*, *teach* and *promise*. These can be drilled when they occur in this pattern in reading-texts.

Once more it is advisable to start with sequences in which no change of tense is needed in the clause.

I got up at ˉhalf past ˎsix this morning. I had breakfast at ˉseven o'ˎclock. I came to school by ˎbus. I got to school at ˉten (minutes) to ˎeight.

ˉWhat time did ˎyou get up this morning, Joan? (I got up at ˉsix o'ˎclock.) ˉWhat time did you have ˎbreakfast? (I had breakfast at a ˉquarter to ˎseven.) ˉDid you ˏwalk to school? (ˎYes, | I ˎdid, *or* ˎNo, | I came to school by ˎbus.) ˉWhat time did you get to ˎschool? (I got to school at ˉfive (minutes) to ˎeight.)

Now make statements with *tell*.

ˉWhat did I ˎtell you, | a ˉminute or two aˎgo? I told you that I got up at ˉhalf past ˎsix. I told you that I had breakfast at ˉseven o'ˎclock. I told you that I came to school by ˎbus. I told you that I got to school at ˉten to ˎeight.

ˉWhat did ˎJoan tell us? She told us that she got up at ˉsix o'ˎclock. (*etc.*, *etc.*)

If you avoid sequences in which changes of tenses are involved, this new pattern for *tell* will soon be mastered. Require pupils to use sequences like those given above until they can do so confidently. Changes from Past Tense to Past Perfect (as in '*I saw* Smith *yesterday*' —'*He* told me that *he had seen* Smith *the previous day*'), with changes of adverbials, *etc.*, are better dealt with by means of written exercises at a later stage.

CHAPTER FIVE (§§ 40–46)

CAN, COULD; BE ABLE TO

§ **40.** *Can* and *can't* were presented in *Stage Two*, §§ 45–52. They were used to denote ability arising from physical strength or capacity, as in 'I can lift this box', with verbs of perception, as in 'I can see some men in the garden', and to indicate possibility, as in 'We can buy things with money'. The form *could* was not presented because of difficulties in its use.[1] We now have to deal with *can* to indicate ability arising from knowledge, as in 'You can speak English', the use of *be able*, and to illustrate some but not all of the uses of *could*.[2]

§ **41.** Start with a revision of the material in Chapter Seven of *Stage Two*. Pay careful attention to the pronunciation of *can* and *can't* as transcribed in § 46, *Stage Two*. Then give examples of *can* to indicate ability arising from knowledge.

You know a ⁻lot of ↘English now, | ↘don't you? You can /kən/ speak English ↘well. You can /kən/ ↘read English well. ⁻Can /kan/ you speak (Chi↗nese)? ↘No, | you ↘can't /ka:nt/.

⁻Could /kud/ you speak English four ↗years ago? ↘No, | you ↘couldn't /'kudnt/. ⁻Could you speak ↗***[3] four years ago? ↘Yes, | you ↘could /kud/. *** is ↘your language. It isn't a ↘foreign language, | ↘is it?

⁻Could you ↗read English four years ago? ↘No, | you ↘couldn't. ⁻Could you read ↗*** four years ago? ↘Yes, | you ↘could.

---

[1] See *A Guide to Patterns and Usage*, § 118.

[2] The use of *could* in conditional sentences is dealt with in Chapter Fifteen of this book.

[3] Give the name of the native language of your pupils.

You probably know which of your pupils are good at athletics and games. Continue by asking questions about these.

ˉCan you ⌐swim, Tom? (⌐Yes, | I ⌐can.) ˉCould you swim when you were ⌐five? (⌐No, | I ⌐couldn't, *or* ⌐Yes, | I ⌐could.) Can /kən/ ˉyou ⌐run well, Roger? (⌐Yes, | I ⌐can.) ˉCould you run well when you were only ⌐eight? (⌐Yes, | I ⌐could, *or* ⌐No, | I ⌐couldn't.) (*etc., etc.*)

If you have girls, you may be able to ask about other kinds of ability and skill, if they have the necessary vocabulary items.

Can /kən/ ˉyou ⌐sew, Edith? ˉCould you sew when you were ⌐eight? (*etc., etc.*)

§ 42. The use of *could* with verbs of perception[1] needs careful treatment. You must, for the present, avoid situations which involve conditions. 'Could you see if I put something over your eyes?' is conditional, and this has not yet been taught. You may, however, use *could see* (*hear*) in sentences with adverbial clauses of past time. Here are some procedures:

ˉCan you see this ⌐ball, Edith? (⌐Yes, | I ⌐can.) I'm going to put the ball in this ⌐box. ˉCan you see it ⌐now? (⌐No, | I ⌐can't.) I'm going to take the ball ⌐out. ˉCan you see it ⌐now? (⌐Yes, | I ⌐can.) ˉCould you see it when it was in the ⌐box? (⌐No, | I ⌐couldn't.)

ˉCan you ⌐see me now, Helen? (⌐Yes, | I ⌐can.) ˉTurn ⌐round, Helen. ˉFace the back ⌐wall.[2] ˉCan you see me ⌐now? (⌐No, | I ⌐can't.) ˉTurn ⌐round again, Helen. ˉFace ⌐me, please. ˉCan you see me ⌐now? (⌐Yes, | I ⌐can.) ˉCould you see me when you faced the ⌐wall? (⌐No, | I ⌐couldn't.)

[1] As in *Stage Two*, §§ 46–49.

[2] Translate this if the verb *face* is not understood.

Pupils should now take over from you, and put questions of this kind to their classmates.

§ 43. In the sentences used in the last section, the form *could* was possible for past time (with no possibility of conditional use) because there were adverbial clauses of time indicating the past (when the ball *was* in the box; when you *faced* the wall). Here are further examples of *could* for past time, with this past time clearly indicated by the situation.[1] Call out two pupils, one small and light (David), the other big and heavy (Paul).

ˇDavid, | ˉtry to lift ˇPaul. ˉCan you ⁄lift him? (ˇNo, | I ˇcan't.) ˉWhy can't you ˇlift him? He's very ˇheavy, *or* He's too ˇheavy for me to lift.[2] ˇThank you, | ˉgo back to your ˇseats.

Now address the whole class.

ˉWhy couldn't David lift ˇPaul? Because Paul is ˉtoo ˇheavy. David ˇtried to lift Paul. He tried ˇhard. But he ˇcouldn't lift him, | because Paul is too ˇheavy.

Note that it is correct in these statements to use *is* instead of *was* (because Paul's weight is unchanged). The whole sequence of questions and statements is essential here to make the situation clear. If you say, 'Could David lift Paul?' outside this sequence, apart from the context, the question would be conditional: 'Could David lift Paul if he tried?' This use of *could* must not be presented at this stage. It would confuse your pupils.

§ 44. *Can* may refer to future time, as in 'Can you come to my house tomorrow?' meaning, 'Will you be free to come? Will circumstances allow you to come?' This use of *can* need not be dealt with until examples occur in reading-texts. When they do occur, you may illustrate the use of *could* for past time, again in contexts that clearly show that past time is being referred to. For example:

[1] For fuller examples see *Stage Two*, §§ 79–80, and the drawings on p. 56.
[2] As in *Stage Two*, § 81.

˜Can you lend me a ⌐dictionary?

After *say* or *tell;*

He said (*or* told me) he ˜couldn't lend me a ⌐dictionary.

Note that the question, 'Could you lend me a dictionary?' (if used in isolation) does not refer to past time. It is an inquiry or a request referring to present or future time.

§ **45.** *Can* is a defective verb. It has no infinitive and no participles. For past and future time *be able to* is often used. When you need to present the use of *be able to* the kind of sequence given below may be useful. It recalls and practises adverbs of manner (as in Chapter Two of this book).

˜Do you speak English ⌐well now? ⌐Yes, | you ⌐do.
˜Were you able to speak English well three ⌐years ago? ⌐No, | you ⌐weren't. You spoke English only a ⌐little then. Next ⌐year | you'll be able to speak English ˜much ⌐better. You'll know a ˜lot ⌐more[1] English.

˜Can David lift this ⌐table? ⌐No, | he ⌐can't. He's not ⌐strong enough. When he's ⌐bigger, | he'll be ⌐stronger. He'll be able to lift the table ⌐easily.

˜Was David able to lift ⌐Paul?[2] ⌐No, | he ⌐wasn't. He ˜wasn't ⌐able to lift Paul. Paul was too ⌐heavy for him to lift.

Perhaps there is, among your pupils, one whose sight is poor and who is going to have glasses. If not, you may talk about an imaginary person.

Tom[3] can't ⌐see well. His ⌐eyes aren't very good. He's

---

[1] This use of *a lot more* may need translation. Do not stop to discuss it at this stage.

[2] This question should follow a repetition of the sequence in § 43 above.

[3] *Or* My friend Smith.

going to have ˅glasses. When he gets his ˊglasses, | he'll be able to ˅see well.

If there are school examinations near, these provide suitable material.

ˉWhen are your next exami˅nations? (They're in ˅June.) ˉAre you ˊworking hard? ˉShall (*or* ˉWill) you be able to ˊpass them?

If there have been examinations in the recent past, show pupils that the Simple Past Tense is the usual one when they are talked about.

ˉWhen were your last exami˅nations? (They were in ˅March.) ˉDid you ˊpass, Mary? (˅Yes, | I ˅did.)

The purpose of these questions is to provide examples of what is correct. Pupils may, without such examples, make the error of saying, 'I *could* pass the examination last March'.

§ 46. When *used to* × *infinitive* has been presented, give examples of *used to be able to* /juːstə bi eibl/ for past time. You may talk about yourself, or, if you do not care to do this, about someone else, real or imaginary.

When I was ˊyoung,[1] | I used to be able to ˅run well. Now I ˅can't run well. (I'm too ˅old.)

When Mr X lived in ˊFrance, | he used to be able to speak ˅French well. That was a ˉlong time a˅go. Now he ˅can't speak French well.

As your pupils make progress in their knowledge of English it requires more ingenuity to find situations suitable for the presentation of new teaching items. Classroom situations are often unsatisfactory or impossible. But the use of your imagination will often provide

[1] *Or* When Mr X, *or* my friend Y, *etc.*

solutions to difficult problems. The presentation of a new teaching item in a situation usually helps much more effectively than the (perhaps easier) approach of giving an explanation in the mother tongue, with translation as an aid. The second approach is often useful, but it should supplement the more lively method of providing a situation.

CHAPTER SIX (§§ 47–52)

INFINITIVES OF PURPOSE
INFINITIVES AFTER NOUNS

§ 47. You have been using questions with *why* and answers with *because* for a long time. Some questions with *why* are answered by the use of infinitives. Here are suggestions for using procedures presenting this use of infinitives.

Start from what is already known and go on to what is new.

ˉWhy do you come to ˅school? You come to school because you want to ˅learn things. You come to school to ˅learn things.[1] You come here to learn ˅English, | ˅history,| ˅science, | and ˉmathe˅matics.

ˉWhy do ˅I come to school every day? I come here to ˅teach you. I come here to give you ˅English lessons.

ˉWhy does Mr (˅X) come here every day? He comes here to give you (˅history) lessons. He comes here to teach you (˅history).

ˉCome to the ˅blackboard, Tom. ˅Clean it, please. ˅Paul, | ˉhelp Tom to clean the ˅blackboard.

Put questions to the class while the blackboard is being cleaned.

ˉWhat's Tom ˅doing? (He's cleaning the ˅blackboard.) ˉWho's ˅helping Tom? (˅Paul is.) ˉWhat's Paul helping Tom to ˅do? (He's helping him to clean the ˅blackboard.)

Then continue with infinitives of purpose. Answer your own questions.

[1] This is VP 25A in *A Guide to Patterns and Usage.*

⁻Why did ↘Tom go to the blackboard? He went to the blackboard to ↘clean it. ⁻Why did ↘Paul go to the blackboard? He went to ⁻help ↘Tom.

Give further examples, using sequences that require vocabulary items with which your pupils are familiar.

I went to the ↘post-office yesterday afternoon. ⁻Why did I ↘go there? I went to buy some ↘stamps.

I went to the ↘cinema last week. ⁻Why did I ↘go there? I went to see a ↘film.[1]

I listen to the ↘radio every evening. ⁻Why do I listen to the ↘radio? I listen because I want to know the ↘news. I listen to the radio to hear the ↘news.

Now put questions for the class to answer.

⁻Why do you come to ↘school, Mary? (I come to school to ↘learn things.) ⁻Why do ↘I come to school, Edith? (You come here to ↘teach us, *or* to give us ↘lessons.)

Pupils may be asked to repeat some of the sequences you have used and to put questions to their classmates. If there is hesitation or error give further examples yourself.

§ 48. Your pupils are familiar with the use of *for* to indicate purpose, as in 'We use scissors for cutting paper and string' and in 'This jug is for milk.'[2] Either now, or when examples first occur in reading-texts, you may present another use of *for* to indicate purpose. Talk about your cat or dog (real or fictional).

I have a ↘cat. Yesterday evening my cat wanted to go ↘out. ⁻What did I ↘do? I opened the ↘door. I ⁻opened the door for the cat to go ↘out.

[1] Or give the title of the film if it is likely to be known.
[2] See *Stage Two*, §§ 115–119.

If in your school it is usual to ring a bell either before school starts in the morning or at the end of a mid-morning break, make use of this fact. It provides a real situation.

⁻Why does the ↘bell ring at (a quarter to eight) every morning? It rings for you to come to ↘school, | ↘doesn't it?

Or ⁻Why does the ↘bell ring, | at the ⁻end of your morning ↘break? It rings for you to ⁻come back into the ↘classroom.

Try to devise other sequences that are easily demonstrated. You may, for example, bring pictures or objects to the classroom, perhaps for teaching new words.

⁻Why did I bring these ↘pictures to the classroom this morning? I brought them here to ↘show you. I brought them here for ⁻you to ↘see. I brought them here to ⁻help you to learn some new ↘words.

§ 49. Infinitives may be used after nouns, and after the pronouns *something*, *anything* and *nothing*. Here are procedures for presenting this teaching item. Start with what is familiar.

I want to ⁻write a ↘letter. ⁻What must I have if I want to write a ↘letter?[1] I must have ↘paper. I must have a ↘pen, | or a ↘pencil. I have ⁻no ↘paper to write on. I have ⁻no ↘pen to write with. I have no ↘pencil to write with. ↘Paul, | will ⁻you give me some ↗paper, please? ↘Thank you. ↘John, | will ⁻you please lend me your ↗pen. ↘Thank you Now I have some ↘paper to write on. I have a ↘pen, | to ↘write with. Now I can /kən/ write a ↘letter. When I had no ↗paper, | and no ↗pen, | I ↘couldn't /'kudnt/ write a letter.[2] Now I ↘can /kan/ write a letter.

[1] This recalls and revises the material in *Stage Two*, Chapter Ten.

[2] Do not neglect to recall recently learnt items. This use of *could* is from the preceding chapter.

Call a pupil to the front. See that he is without paper, pen, or pencil. Then ask questions.

¯Have you any ⌃paper to write on, David? ⌄Long answer, please.[1] (⌄No, | I have ⌄no paper to write on.) ¯Has David a ⌃pen to write with, Paul? ⌄Long answer, please. (⌄No, | he ⌄hasn't a pen to write with.)

Repeat with other pupils, using other situations.

⌄Look, Mary, I have a piece of ⌄wood here. I want you to ⌄cut it. ¯Have you a ⌃knife, | to ⌃cut it with? (⌄No, | I ⌄haven't.) ¯Why can't you cut the ⌄wood, Mary? (Because I ¯haven't a ⌄knife.)

⌄Susan, | I have a piece of ⌄paper (⌄string) here. I want you to ⌄cut it. ¯Have you any ⌃scissors (*or* a pair of ⌃scissors), | to ⌃cut it with? (⌄No, | I ⌄haven't.) ⌄Here's a pair of scissors to cut it with. ¯Can you cut the paper ⌃now, Susan? (⌄Yes, | I ⌄can.)

Require pupils to repeat these sequences, making the statements and requests, and asking questions for their classmates to answer.

§ 50. Next use *something*, *anything* and *nothing*.

¯Is there anything to ⌃eat on this table? ⌄No, | there ⌄isn't. There's ⌄nothing to eat on this table. ⌄Look, | I have ¯something in this ⌄box. It's a ⌄biscuit.[1] Now there's ¯something to ⌄eat on the table.

Repeat the sequence and require pupils to answer your questions. Repeat with *drink*.[3] Perhaps one of your pupils is silent when you ask a question. In this case you may comment:

[1] You require the long answer so that the new item is repeated and practised.

[2] Or apple, or whatever you can supply.

[3] Produce a glass of water or milk, or a bottle of Coca-cola.

He ⁻hasn't answered (*or* ⁻can't answer) my ⌄question. He has ⁻nothing to ⌄say.

Other examples that you may use from time to time during the next few weeks are:

⁻Do I give you too much ∕homework to do? ⁻Have I given you any ∕homework to do? ⁻Have you any interesting ∕books to read?

The occasional use of a new item in this way is useful and valuable. It serves to keep in mind an item on which, perhaps, you have been able to spend only a few minutes on its first presentation. If, when the class is busy with written exercises, you find a pupil apparently idle, you may say:

⁻Haven't you anything to ∕do, John? Have you ⁻finished your work al∕ready?

§ 51. There are many other examples of nouns used with following infinitives which you can present to your class incidentally, not in a special presentation. From now on, whenever opportunities occur, use some of the following:

At the end of a lesson:

It's (ten) o'⌄clock. It's time to ⌄stop now, | ⌄isn't it?

If a pupil makes a spelling error while writing on the blackboard:

⁻Is ∕that the way[1] to spell the word (*or* to spell *arrive*)? *Or* ⁻Is that the ∕right way to spell the word *colour*?

If a pupil mispronounces a word:

⁻Is that the ∕right way to pronounce this word?[2] ⌄No, | it ⌄isn't. ⁻What's the right way to pro⌄nounce it, Paul?

---

[1] Perhaps this is the first use of *way* in this meaning. If so, translate your question.

[2] Write the word on the blackboard.

After giving an explanation of a new passage of reading:

ˉHave you any ⌄questions to ask? *Or* ˉHas anyone a ⌄question to ask?

§ 52. Your pupils have learnt the use of adjectives followed by infinitives.[1] They have heard and used such sentences as:

This word is ˉeasy (ˉhard, ˉdifficult) to ⌄spell. Some questions are ˉdifficult to ⌄answer.

When pupils have mastered the material in § 49, you may occasionally let them hear examples of a pattern closely related to it. Instead of 'This chair is comfortable to sit on', we may say 'This is a comfortable chair to sit on'.[2] Present this pattern incidentally, not as a 'set' lesson. Here are suggestions:

After your pupils have heard many examples of 'Was that question easy to answer?' use, without comment, 'Was that an easy question to answer?'

If you are fortunate enough to have a pleasant classroom, you may remark, quite casually: 'This room is pleasant to work in, isn't it?' And then, 'This is a pleasant room to work in'. In both statements the infinitive phrase refers to the adjective, although in one case the adjective is used attributively and in the other predicatively. You should not, however, give these grammatical terms to your pupils.

---

[1] See § 34 in Chapter Three of this book.
[2] See *A Guide to Patterns and Usage*, § 82g.

CHAPTER SEVEN (§§ 53–62)

MORE PREPOSITIONAL USAGES
OVER, ABOVE, ACROSS, UNDER, BELOW

§ **53.** Many of the most frequently used prepositions have been dealt with already. As your pupils make progress in their English studies they will meet new prepositions in their reading-texts. They will also find that many of the prepositions they have already met are used in new ways.

It is undesirable to give specially prepared lessons on prepositions. When a new preposition occurs, or when a preposition occurs with a new or different meaning, a few minutes may be devoted to examples and drills. You should not, therefore, present the material in this chapter as a 'lesson'. Use the cumulative index of structural words at the end of this book and present the material here as the need for it arises.

§ **54.** *Over* usually occurs at an early stage in an English course. It will occur, probably, in contexts where it is contrasted with *on* and *under*.[1] Recall and practise the uses with which your pupils are already familiar. Then present *above* and make clear, through examples, when *above* and *over* are interchangeable and when they are not.

Make a simple blackboard sketch of a table, with an electric lamp hanging from the ceiling *over* the table. Draw something (e.g. a basket) *on* the table, and something (e.g. a box, a dog) on the floor *under* the table. As this is not new material you may put questions to the class at once, without preliminary statements.

¯Where's the ↘lamp? (It's ¯over the ↘table.) ¯Where's the ↘box. (It's ↘under the table.) (*etc., etc.*)

Now present the new word *above*.

[1] See *Stage One*, §§ 84–85.

The lamp's ‾over the ⌄table. It's a⌄bove the table.

You may tell the class that the two words have the same meaning here and that either may be used. You may point out that the lamp and the table are separated in space, that they are not touching.

§ 55. Next place a jacket, raincoat, or other article of clothing across the top of a chair, and make the statements:

‾Where did I put my ⌄coat? I put it ‾over the ⌄chair (*or* ‾over the back of the ⌄chair, *or* ‾over the arm of the ⌄chair).

Contrast *over* and *on*. Place the coat on the seat (not the back or arms) of the chair.

‾Where's the coat ⌄now? It's on the ⌄seat of the chair. ‾Come ⌄here, Paul. ‾Put this coat on that ⌄desk. ‾Where have you put the ⌄coat? (I've put it on the ⌄desk.) ‾Now put it over the back of the ⌄chair. ‾Where has Paul put the ⌄coat, David? (He's put it ‾over the back of the ⌄chair.)

Require other pupils to make similar requests and ask questions while you listen.

§ 56. You may, if you wish, point out[1] that *over*, in the kind of situation just illustrated, indicates 'on the surface of and covering, partly or completely'. You may then give further examples. Perhaps you can show a jar.

‾Look at this ⌄jar. ‾Is there a ⌁lid on it? (⌄No, | there ⌄isn't.) I'm going to ‾tie this piece of ⌄paper over it. ‾What am I ⌄doing now? I'm ‾tying this piece of paper over the top of the ⌄jar.[2]

[1] In the language of your pupils.

[2] You may say 'over the *mouth* of the jar' if you wish.

Call a pupil to the front and place a large-size hat on his head. Then give the hat a push so that it falls over his eyes. Take the opportunity of revising *too*.

¯Look at this ⌄hat. It's a ⌄large hat, | ⌄isn't it? It's ¯too ⌄large for you, | ⌄isn't it? ¯What have I just ⌄done? I've ¯pushed the hat over Tom's ⌄eyes. Tom can't ⌄see now, | ⌄can he? The hat's ¯over his ⌄eyes.

Other possibilities are spreading a handkerchief over your face (or the face of one of your pupils) (perhaps with the comment 'to keep the flies off',[1] thus recalling the infinitive of purpose dealt with in Chapter Six), spreading a newspaper over the top of a desk or small table (perhaps with the comment 'to keep it clean'[1] before you proceed to the next activity), pouring sand from a box or bag over some pebbles or other small objects. Make statements while you perform the actions and then put questions to the class (either Past Tense, or Present Perfect with *just*).

¯What have I just ⌄done? (You've ¯spread a ⌄newspaper (*or* a sheet of ⌄newspaper) over the desk.) ¯What have I done ⌄now? (You've put some small ⌄stones on the desk.) ¯What have I just ⌄done, Paul? (You've poured ⌄sand over the stones.) ⌄Yes, | I've ¯covered the stones with ⌄sand.[2]

§ **57.** *Over* may also mean 'from one side of to the other side of'. Aviation provides examples to illustrate the difference between *over* and *above*. Talk in this way.

¯Do airliners fly very ⌄high? (⌄Yes, | they ⌄do.) Airliners often fly a¯bove the ⌄clouds, | ⌄don't they? ¯Do airliners fly over the At⌄lantic? Yes, | they ⌄do. Airliners fly over the Atlantic ¯every ⌄day. They fly from ¯London to New ⌄York. They fly from ⌄Paris to New York.

[1] Probably a new use of the verb *keep*.
[2] This is a useful opportunity for presenting *cover* and for recalling *with*.

§ 58. Compare *over* and *across*.[1] Both may be used in the sense 'from one side of to the other side of'. If a stream is very narrow, it is possible to jump *over* it, or *across it*. If the stream is wide, it may be impossible to jump *over* it, but possible to swim *across* it.

Another common use of *over* is 'in every part of'. Give a few examples when *over* occurs in reading-texts in this sense.

‾Is Mr X[2] famous only in ⌐this country (*or* in ⌐India, *etc.*) | or ‾is he famous all over the ⌐world?

I have (Mr X has) travelled ‾all over this ⌐country (‾all over ⌐Asia, *etc.*).

§ 59. The use of *over* for 'more than' is easy to understand and easy to illustrate. Only a few examples will be needed. *Over* may be contrasted with *under*.

‾How ⌐old are the pupils in this class? You are ‾all over (⌐twelve). ‾How old am ⌐I? You don't ⌐know, | ⌐do you. ‾Am I over ⌐twenty?[3] (⌐Yes, | you ⌐are.) ‾Am I over (⌐sixty)? (⌐No, | you're ⌐not.) I'm ‾over (⌐twenty) | and I'm ‾under (⌐sixty).

‾How long is the river (⌐X)? ‾Is it a ⌐thousand miles long? (⌐No, | it ⌐isn't.) ‾How long ⌐is it? I don't ⌐know. It's ‾over ⌐eighty miles. Perhaps it's a ⌐hundred miles long.

§ 60. *Under* and *below* form another pair that need illustration. Start by recalling the uses of *under* with which your pupils are familiar.[4]

‾Look at these two ⌐books. ‾Where's the ⌐red book? It's ‾under the ⌐blue book.

[1] See *Stage Two*, § 173.

[2] Give the name of a statesman or other person whose name is familiar.

[3] Supply whatever figures you wish in this sequence.

[4] See *Stage One*, §§ 84–85.

⁻Look at this ↘drawing. ⁻Is there a ↗saucer under the cup? (↘Yes, | there ↘is.) (*etc., etc.*)

§ 61. Next give examples of *below*. Draw a line on the blackboard.

↘Edith, | ⁻come to the ↘blackboard, please. ⁻Write your name on this ↘line. ⁻Where has Edith just written her ↘name, Susan? (She's written it on the ↘line.) ↘Mary, | ⁻come and write your name a↘bove the line. ⁻Where has ↘Mary written her name? (She's written it a↘bove the line.) I'm going to write my name be↘low the line. ↘Look, | my name's be↘low the line.

Use the examples in § 59 about age, this time using *below* instead of *under*.

There are ⁻no children in this class below (↘ten), | ↘are there?

Draw a line on the blackboard to represent the horizon (and give your pupils this word). Then draw a circle to represent the sun and say:

The sun is a⁻bove the ho↘rizon now. When the sun ↗sets,[1] | it goes be↘low the horizon.

Under is not used in this context.

§ 62. Another useful association for *above* and *below* is with temperatures. You may make a simple blackboard sketch of a thermometer and mark on it freezing-point (0°C.) and boiling-point (100° C.).[2] Then indicate various points on the scale and ask:

⁻Is this point a↗bove freezing-point | or be↘low freezing-point?

---

[1] The use of *rise* and *set* is presented in *Stage One*, §§ 169–172.

[2] Note, in these compounds, the stress pattern: stress on the gerund only.

If the words *ice* and *steam* are known (or if you have time to present them), you may use these questions:

⁻When does water change into ⌄ice? It changes into ⌃ice | when the ⁻temperature is at ⌄freezing-point, | or be⌄low freezing-point. ⁻When does it change into ⌄steam? It changes into ⌃steam | when the temperature is at ⌄boiling-point, | or a⌄bove boiling-point.

Another useful association is with the noun *level*, especially in *sea level*.[1]

⁻How high is this town above sea ⌄level? It's ⁻(fifty) ⌄metres above sea level. ⁻Are there any parts of the world be⌃low sea level? (⌄Yes, | there ⌄are.) ⁻Are there any ⌃coal-mines (⌃gold-mines, *etc.*) in this country? ⌄Yes, | there ⌄are. Some of them are ⁻five hundred metres below the ⌄ground (the ⌄surface).

Note that when we refer to measures of distance in these contexts, *above* and *below* are used, not *over* and *under*.

You will not use this material until your pupils have the necessary vocabulary. It is, however, important that they should learn prepositional usages in association with those words with which they are regularly used. So if they hear from you such examples as *above* (*below*) *freezing-point* (*sea level, the horizon*), they will be learning the prepositions in the right way, not in isolation but in use.

[1] Equal stresses: 'sea 'level.

CHAPTER EIGHT (§§ 63–70)

IF-CLAUSES (1)

§ **63.** *If*-clauses are of great variety.[1] Your pupils are by now familiar with those in which the Simple Present Tense is used in both the subordinate and the main clause.[2] In this chapter procedures are suggested for dealing with clauses referring to future time, and clauses referring to unfulfilled or impossible conditions.

Start with what is familiar, statements with *can*. Then, for *can*, use *shall/will be able to*.[3]

‾What can you ↘do, Tom, | if you have a piece of ↘chalk? (I can write on the ↘blackboard.) ‾Have ↗you any chalk, David? (↘No, | I ↘haven't.) ‾What will David be able to ↘do, | if I ↘give him a piece of chalk? He'll be able to write on the ↘blackboard, | ↗won't he?

‾What can you do if you have a ↘knife, Paul? (I can ↘cut things.) ↘Look, | ↘here's a knife. ‾What will Paul be able to ↘do, | if I ‾give him this ↘knife, | and this piece of ↘wood? He'll be able to ↘cut this piece of wood, | ↗won't he?

‾Look at this ↘box (↘bag). It has a ↘lock. This is the ↘key. ‾What will John be able to ↘do, | if I give him the ↘key? He'll be able to ↘open the box (bag).

In these sequences you have been recalling and revising the use of *shall/will be able to*. You have also been using questions that are much longer than those you normally ask. These longer questions may need to be divided into intonation phrases. It is possible to say:

‾What will John be able to do if I give him this ↘key?

---

[1] See *A Guide to Patterns and Usage*, § 119 (pp. 231–237), for a fairly full treatment.

[2] See *Stage Two*, Chapter Ten.

[3] As presented in §§ 45–46 of this book.

Such an utterance requires fairly rapid speech. A slower (and, for your pupils, an easier) utterance would be:

ˉWhat will John be able to ˅do, | if I ˉgive him this ˅key?

The slight pause after *do* (with its fall in pitch) will help your pupils to follow the long question more easily.

ˉWhat will Paul be able to ˅do, | if I give him this ˅knife, | and this piece of ˅wood?

This question of eighteen words is broken up into three parts, with pauses after *do* and *knife*.

Note that in the examples so far given the tone symbols indicate a fall in pitch on the word in the *if*-clause to which most prominence is given (e.g. *chalk*, *knife*, *key*). It is possible to have a rise in pitch on these words in statements, as is shown in § 64. In questions, follow the indications (as given by arrows) in the examples.

As this new material requires considerable concentration, give further examples before you require pupils to answer questions.[1] Then repeat some of them and put questions to the class.

ˉWhat will you be able to ˅do, Paul, | if I ˉgive you this piece of ˅chalk? (I'll be able to ˉwrite on the ˅blackboard.)

ˉWhat will ˅Mary be able to do, | if I ˉgive her this ˅key? (She'll be able to ˉopen that ˅box.)

Then require pupils to ask questions to be answered by their classmates.

§ 64. The examples in this section may be used before those in the last section if you prefer. They probably require the use of words that your pupils have not yet learnt. Those in § 63 use words already known. The verb *happen* is useful. Give the equivalent in the language of your pupils.

ˉWhat's ˅this? It's a ˅tennis ball, | ˅isn't it? If I ˉpress this ball ∕hard, | it will ˉchange its ˅shape. ˅Look, | I'm ˅pressing the ball. It has ˉchanged its ˅shape.

[1] Use any of the sequences in §§ 73–74, *Stage Two*.

Note that the *if*-clause here is placed first. (In § 63 the *if*-clauses are in questions, and all follow the main clauses.) Note, too, that there is a rise in pitch on the word that is made prominent in the clause.

If I ‾press the ball /hard, . . .

Do not comment on this. Intonation patterns are very varied. Your wisest plan at present is to follow the indications given by the tone symbols. The patterns indicated here are those most suitable for classroom presentation of the material: a rise in pitch in an *if*-clause that comes first, and a fall in pitch in an *if*-clause when it comes at the end. The rise in pitch normally indicates an incomplete statement.

‾What's ˅this? (It's a piece of ˅chalk.) I'm going to ˅drop it. ‾What ˅happened? The piece of chalk ˅broke, | ˅didn't it?

After dealing, if necessary, with the words *happen* and *broke*, hold up a glass (or other fragile object).

‾What's ˅this? (It's a ˅glass.) ‾If I drop this /glass, | it will ˅break, | ˅won't it? I don't ˅want to break the glass. I'm not ˅going to drop it.

Repeat this sequence with the *if*-clause at the end.

‾What's ˅this? ˅This is a glass, | ˅too. ‾What will ˅happen, | if I ˅drop it? (*Or* ‾What will happen if I ˅drop it?[1]) It will ˅break, | ˅won't it?

‾What's ˅this? (It's a piece of ˅wood.) ‾What will happen if I drop this piece of ˅wood? ‾Will it /break, Paul? (˅No, | it ˅won't.)

§ **65.** The weather in Great Britain is uncertain. It changes often. When, therefore, people make statements about plans that are dependent upon the weather, they often qualify them by saying 'if

[1] As the question is short it may be uttered without a pause.

it rains tomorrow', or 'if it's fine', or 'if the weather's good'. Your country may be one where there is no such uncertainty. You may have a long dry season and a predictable rainy season. If, however, your weather is, like that of Great Britain, variable, you may like to use the sequences suggested here.

‾Will it ∕rain tomorrow? I don't ∖know. Perhaps it ∕will (*or* ∖will); perhaps it ∖won't. If it ∕rains tomorrow, | I shall use my um∖brella. ‾Will ∕you use an umbrella if it rains tomorrow, Paul? (∖Yes, | I ∖will, *or* ∖No, | I ∖won't.)

Make statements about what you are likely to do on Sunday (or any other day that is a holiday). Then put questions to your pupils.

If it's ∕fine on Sunday (*or* If it doesn't ∕rain on Sunday), | I shall go to the ‾sea∖side (the ∖mountains, *etc.*).[1] If it ∕isn't fine on Sunday (*or* If it ∕rains on Sunday), | I ∖shan't go to the seaside. I shall perhaps go to the ∖cinema (stay at ∖home, read a ∖book, *etc.*).

‾What will ∖you do, Paul, | if it's ∖fine on Sunday? ‾What will you do if it ∖rains?

During the earlier stages of the English course your questions were usually such that only one answer (on the facts, not the grammatical correctness!) was possible. Now, however, a wide variety of answers is possible to some questions. Your pupils have not reached the stage of 'free conversation'. It is still 'controlled or guided oral work'. But the wider range of possible answers is an indication of progress. It makes the oral work more attractive.

§ 66. There are numerous other ways in which this new material may be presented. One of the most effective ways of helping pupils to become familiar with a new item is to use it incidentally from time to time. You may make statements such as these:

If you ∕work well, | I shall be ∖happy (∖pleased). ‾If you all ∕work hard, | you'll ‾pass the exami∖nation next month.

[1] Or the name of any local resort known to your pupils.

If you ⸴don't work hard, | you ⸜won't pass the examination.
You'll ⸜fail in the examination.[1]

You may be able to refer to games.

⁻If our team plays ⸴well, | we shall ⸜win the match
against (X).

§ 67. The next step (perhaps two or three weeks later) is to present
examples of unfulfilled conditions (unlikely, impossible, contrary to
fact). There is again a wide variety of possible tense sequences, and
at this stage it is desirable to restrict your examples. The sequences
below are restricted to sentences in which there is a Past Tense in the
if-clause. In the main clause the finites *would*, *should* and *could* are
used with infinitives.

⁻Look at this ⸜glass. If I ⸴dropped it, | it would ⸜break.
I'm not ⸜going to drop it.

⁻Look at this piece of ⸜chalk. If I ⸴dropped it, | it would
⸜break. I've ⸜dropped it. ⁻What ⸜happened? It ⸜broke.
It broke into ⁻two (⁻three) ⸜pieces.

⁻What would Mary ⸜say, | if I ⁻gave her these ⸜flowers?
She would say '⸜Thank you'. ⁻What would ⸜you say,
Joan, if I gave you these flowers?[2] You would say '⸜Thank
you', | ⸜wouldn't you?

Use the weak forms of *would* in the questions.

It would ⸜break.	/it wəd breik/
She would say . . .	/ʃi: wəd sei/
You would say . . .	/ju: wəd sei/

---

[1] If this use of *pass* and *fail in* is new, repeat several times and require
pupils to write in their notebooks: *I passed the examination. Two boys
failed in the examination.* In this way they will have a record of *fail* with
the preposition *in*. Children in Great Britain shorten *examination* to *exam*.
You may like to give your pupils this shortened form and encourage
them to use it.

[2] Fall in pitch on *you*, with the rest of the question on a low level pitch.

For *wouldn't,* in the tag-question, the strong form is used.

, wouldn't you?   /, ˎwudnt juː/

After several repetitions, use *she'd* /ʃiːd/, *he'd* /hiːd/, and *you'd* /juːd/. Write *would,* and the forms *she'd, he'd,* and *you'd* on the blackboard, to show the spelling forms.

§ 68. With the first person pronouns *I* and *we* you may present either *would* or *should.* Your choice may be decided for you by a Syllabus, or by the textbooks you use. The form *I'd* /aid/ is common in speech, but in writing a choice has to be made between *would* and *should,* and, of course, in questions. Here are sequences with *should.*

ˉWhat should I ˎsay, | if you ˎgave me something? I should (*or* I'd) say 'ˎThank you', | ˎshouldn't I?

ˉLook at that big ˎtree, | in the ˎgarden. ˉIf I tried to climb that ˏtree, | I should ˎfall, perhaps, | and ˎhurt myself.

When you put questions to the class it is advisable to use familiar material. So use the sequences from §§ 63–64 again, with the necessary changes. With the first use of *could,* however, you must answer the questions yourself.

ˉWhat could I ˎdo, | if I had a piece of ˎchalk? I could ˉwrite on the ˎblackboard.

Repeat with *knife* and *key.* Use the weak form of *could* /kəd/ in questions. In short answers and in tag-questions use the strong forms /kud/ and /kud(nt)/.

Here are questions to be put to the class, all based on material in §§ 63–64.

ˉWhat would Mary be able to ˎdo, | if I ˉgave her this ˎkey? (She'd be able to ˉopen the ˎbox.)

ˉWhat would you be able to ˎdo, John, | if I ˉgave you this ˎknife? (I'd be able to ˉcut the ˎwood.)

ˉWhat should (*or* would) ⌄I be able to do, | if ˉyou gave ⌄me a knife? (⌄You'd be able to cut the wood.)

ˉWhat would happen if I dropped this ⌄glass? (It would ⌄break.)

ˉWhat would happen if I pressed this ⌄tennis-ball? (It would change its ⌄shape.)

ˉWhat could you do if you had a ⌄pen, | and some ⌄paper? (I could write a ⌄letter.)

ˉCould you write a letter if you had a ⌄pencil? (⌄Yes, | I ⌄could.)

§ 69. In the last section the conditions were unfulfilled, but were not unlikely or impossible conditions. In this section there are examples of conditions that are unlikely to be fulfilled, and some that are impossible. The use of *were* for *was* is not essential. Many speakers say 'If I *was* rich'. Here *were* is preferred. This is a survival of the subjunctive mood. There is no need to talk about this in grammatical terms, though you may do so briefly if there is a parallel use in the language of your pupils. For the sums of money in the sequences below, substitute suitably large sums in your own currency (one lakh of rupees, ten thousand dinars, *etc.*).

ˉIf I had (ten thousand ⌄pounds), | I should be a ˉrich ⌄man, | ⌄shouldn't I? I could buy a new ⌄house. I could travel round the ⌄world. (*etc.,etc.*)[1] But I ⌄haven't (ten thousand pounds). I'm ⌄not a rich man. I ⌄can't buy a new house. (*etc.*, *etc.*)

The negative statements are important. They help pupils to understand the kind of condition used here—one that is unfulfilled and improbable.

Use *like* in some of your sequences. This is useful because of the very frequent use of 'I'd like to . . .', 'Would you like to . . .', and other phrases (with an unexpressed condition).

[1] Add whatever the vocabulary of your pupils (and your own imagination) makes possible.

If I were ˅rich, | I'd ˅like to travel round the world. I'd like to go to (˅London, | and ˅Rome, and . . .[1]).

If your pupils are familiar with the English names for peoples of other countries, and the names of the languages spoken in them, this sequence is useful.

⁻If you were a ˅French boy, | ⁻what ˅language would you speak? You'd speak ˅French, | ˅wouldn't you?
⁻What language would you speak if you were a ˅German girl, Mary? You'd speak ˅German, | ˅wouldn't you?
⁻What language should (*or* would) ˅I speak, | if I were an E˅gyptian? I'd speak ˅Arabic. ⁻Should (*or* would) I speak Arabic if I were an I˅raqi? ˅Yes, | I ˅should (*or* ˅would).

These statements and questions are longer than the kind usually found in grammar books (e.g. 'If you were a bird, you could fly'), but are more useful and perhaps more interesting to your pupils.

§ 70. In the last section the verbs in the *if*-clause were limited to *had* and *were*. When question and answer drills show that pupils are ready for the next step, present examples in which other Past Tense forms are used. Suggestions follow.
Start by using the language material again.

⁻If you went to ˅England, | ⁻what ˅language would you speak? You'd speak ˅English, | ˅wouldn't you? ⁻What language would you speak if you went to the United ˅States? You'd speak English ˅there, | ˅wouldn't you? ⁻Would you speak English if you went to ˅Canada? ˅Yes, | you ˅would.

Methods of travel to places abroad can be talked about.

[1] Your personal preferences, of course.

⁻If you went to ⌐London, | ⁻how would you like to
⌐travel? ⁻Would you like to go by ⌐air? ⁻Would you like
to go by ⌐sea?

Journeys in your own town or country will provide material.

⁻How long would it ⌐take you, | if you went from ⁻here
to (X) by ⌐bus (*or* ⌐train)? It would take you (⁻two ⌐hours).

At a later stage you will present unfulfilled conditions in the past.
These will follow the presentation of the Past Perfect Tense. See
Chapter Fifteen below.

CHAPTER NINE (§§ 71–82)

OBLIGATION AND NECESSITY
(AND THEIR OPPOSITES)[1]
MUST; HAVE TO; NEEDN'T; NEED TO;
OUGHT TO; SHOULD

§ **71.** The verb *must* is probably known to your pupils in its most
frequent use. *Must* is used in several senses. In the statement: 'If I
want to buy things, I must have money', it indicates what is necessary.

Recall this use of *must*. Give two or three minutes to statements,
questions and answers.[2] Then give similar statements using *necessary*
in the pattern illustrated in § 33 of this book. Recall statements with
easy, difficult and *(im)possible*, including some with *for me* (*you*, etc.).
For *necessary* use first familiar contexts and then some new ones.

˹If I want to ˏbuy things, | I must have ˎmoney. It's
˹necessary for me to have ˎmoney.

Note the pronunciation of the word, and the weak form of *for*.

its ˹nesisəri fə miː tə hav ˎmʌni.

After two or three repetitions you may say /ˈnesisri/, which is the
usual pronunciation at normal speed.

˹What's it necessary for me to have if I want to ˎwrite?
It's ˹necessary for me to have a ˎpen, | or a ˎpencil.

/its ˹nesisri fə miː tə hav ə ˎpen, | ɔːr ə ˎpensl./

You may give a few other examples of this adjective.

Good ˏfood, | and ˏsleep, | are ˹both necessary to
ˎhealth. ˹Is ˏexercise necessary to health? Perhaps it ˎis.

[1] For a fairly full treatment, see *A Guide to Patterns and Usage*, § 114
(pp. 216–220).

[2] See *Stage Two*, § 76.

§ 72. The next step is to use *necessary* in a slightly different sense, not for something that is essential, but for what is required by custom, rules and regulations, *etc.* This enables you to present the use of *have to* with infinitives.

‾Is it necessary for you to come to school on ⌄Sundays?[1] ⌄No, | it ⌄isn't. It ‾isn't necessary for you to come to school on ⌄Sundays. Sunday's a ⌄holiday, | ⌄isn't it?

‾Is it necessary for you to come to school on Saturday after⌄noons?

Now use *have to*.

You ‾all have to come to school on ⌄Mondays. You ‾all have to come to school on ⌄Tuesdays.

‾What's to⌄day? (It's ⌄Monday.) ‾Will (*or* ‾Shall) you have to come to school to⌄morrow? ⌄Yes, | you ⌄will. (*Or* ⌄No, | you ⌄won't. Tomorrow's a ⌄holiday.) ‾Did you have to come to school ⌄yesterday? ⌄No, | you ⌄didn't, *or* ⌄Yes, | you ⌄did.

Note that in the interrogative and negative the helping verb *do* is used. Give further examples.

At ‾what time do you have to be at ⌄school in the morning? You have to be here at (‾eight o'⌄clock), | ⌄don't you? ⌄I have to be here at eight o'clock, | ⌄too. At ‾what time do I have to get ⌄up, | to be ⌄here at (eight) o'clock? I have to get up at (‾half-past ⌄six).

In the last question you give an example of the infinitive of purpose (*to be here*), presented in Chapter Six, § 47. As the question is long, repeat it two or three times before using it with the name of a pupil who is to answer.

If your pupils know the words *cost* and *pay*, ask questions about

[1] Or perhaps *Fridays* if you are in a Muslim country.

what has to be paid for articles your pupils are likely to buy. Firs
ask and answer questions yourself.

⁻How much do we have to pay for a ↘pencil? We have
to pay (↘fourpence, | or ↘fivepence).[1] ⁻How much do we
have to pay for a good ↘fountain-pen?[2] We have to pay
(⁻five ↘shillings). ⁻How much do we have to pay for a
bottle of Coca-↘cola? (*etc., etc.*)

§ **73.** When pupils use this new item confidently and correctly,
combine it with other items that have been presented recently, for
example, a noun with an infinitive, and *be able to:*

⁻Have you a lot of ↗homework to do this evening, Paul?
(↘Yes, | I ↘have.) ⁻Will you be able to go out and ↗play
this evening, | or ⁻will you have to stay ↘in, | to do your
↘homework? (I'll have to stay ↘in, | to do my ↘homework.)

If Paul answers 'No', you may comment:

You'll be able to go out and ↘play, | ↘won't you?

Other possible sequences, to be used incidentally on suitable
occasions, are:

⁻Will you be able to pass the exami↗nation next month,
Mary?

If Mary answers 'No', you may comment:

You'll have to ↘work hard during the next two or three
weeks, | ↘won't you?

This incidental use of a new teaching item is important. It serves
to prevent it from being forgotten and to show your pupils that what
they are learning is of use in everyday situations.

[1] Give prices in local currency.

[2] Or ⁻ball ↘pen (if these are used by your pupils).

§ 74. If you are in a school where British colloquial usage is considered important (but not otherwise), you may give examples of *have got to* for *have to*.[1] A good opportunity is at a written examination in which pupils are to answer only some of the questions.

There are ⁻ten ⸜questions in this examination. ⁻Have you got to answer ⸍all of them? ⸜No, | you ⸜haven't. You ⁻haven't got to answer ⸜all of them. You have to answer ⁻only ⸜six.

Note that here *have you got to* is used instead of *do you have to*, and *haven't got to* instead of *don't have to*. If you give this usage, do so only after the ordinary (non-colloquial) use has been mastered. This colloquial use with *got* is restricted to the Present. For Future and Past *shall have to* and *had to* (without *got*) are used.

§ 75. Written exercises may be used to follow up the oral work. Provide a number of sentences with *necessary* and require pupils to convert them. The sentences may be written on the blackboard, converted orally, and then done in writing. See that there are examples of present, past, and future. Here are specimens:

It is necessary for us to be there at eight o'clock. (We have to be there . . .)

It will be necessary for them to work hard. (They will have to . . .)

It was necessary for John to leave early. (John had to . . .)

§ 76. *Need* is a verb that involves many teaching problems.[2] It is used with nouns ('I need a new hat'), with infinitives ('Do you need to go so early?'), and with the contracted form of *not* and an infinitive (*needn't*) to indicate absence of necessity ('You needn't do that'). If you present all these uses together your pupils will be confused. So present them one at a time, spaced out at intervals of several weeks or even months. The best plan is to present them as they occur in reading-texts.

[1] Cf. the use of *have got* (*a pen*, etc.) for *have* (*a pen*, etc.), noted in *Stage One*, § 61.

[2] See *A Guide to Patterns and Usage*, § 8.

§ 77. Whereas *don't have to* indicates absence of obligation, *needn't* indicates absence of necessity. The statement 'Men in this country don't have to serve in the Army' indicates that military service is not obligatory or compulsory. The statement 'You needn't come to the office tomorrow' indicates permission to stay away from the office. The question 'Must he come?' means 'Do you require him to come, do you insist upon his coming?'; the question 'Need he come?' asks whether it is necessary for him to come, whether he may be absent. This use of *need*, unchanged for the third person singular, which is *he (she) needn't, need he (she)*, is restricted to the negative and interrogative. In the affirmative *must* or *have to* is used. The affirmative form may occur in dependent questions, as in 'I wonder whether I need go', and with *hardly* and *scarcely*.[1]

§ 78. It is not easy to present this use of *needn't* in oral drills. The problem of finding suitable situations is difficult. You may, however, use *needn't* incidentally when opportunities occur. When you use it for the first time, give a translation of your sentence.

Perhaps you will have written exercises for your class. If the number of questions is small, you may say:

I want you to answer ⁻all these ⌄questions. There are ⁻only ⌄ten. You must (try to) answer ⌄all of them.

On another occasion the number of questions to be answered in writing may be large, or there may not be enough time for pupils to answer all of them. You may say:

You ⁻needn't answer ⌄all these questions. ⁻Answer only numbers one to ⌄ten.

If your pupils have more than one English textbook, you may, for some lessons, use only one of them. This information may be given to the class, using both *must* and *needn't*, a good contrast.

You must ⁻bring your ⌄reading-books tomorrow. You ⁻needn't bring your compo⌄sition books.

---

[1] You are not likely to present these until a later stage, so although you should be aware of the problems involved, you will not deal with them until they arise. Do not give information until it is required.

You may also use *must* in occasional statements, for example, to pupils who are not working as hard as you expect.

You must ˅work harder, Tom, | if you want to pass the exami˅nation.

At the end of a lesson period:

Well, we must ˅stop now. It's ⁻twelve o'˅clock.

§ 79. The use of *need* as an ordinary verb, negative and interrogative forms with the helping verb *do*, and with a noun or pronoun as its object, is probably less important, because less commonly used, than the use of *needn't* as dealt with in the preceding section. The meaning is 'require' or 'want'. Instead of a special presentation with question and answer drills it is better, probably, to use occasional examples during classroom work, with a translation for the first few examples. Here are possible situations for the incidental use of *need* in this sense.

When the class is doing written work, and to pupils who seem to be in doubt or difficulty:

⁻Can't you ⁄answer that question, Tom? Do you ⁻need ⁄help?

When you see a pupil who cannot find a pen or pencil:

⁻Haven't you ⁄started yet, Paul? Do you ⁻need a ⁄pen? ⁻Can't you ⁄find your pen? (*or* Have you ⁻lost your ⁄pen?)

When you see a pupil using a mere stump of a pencil:

That pencil's too ˅short, David. You need a ˅new one.

§ 80. *Need* is also used with *to* and an infinitive, as in 'Do you need to start so early?' and 'I don't need to leave until six.' This is easily confused with the use of *needn't* and an infinitive without *to*, as in 'You needn't go yet, need you?' It is advisable to postpone using examples of *need* in this pattern until examples occur in reading-texts. When you give examples, do so with reference to future time, that is, with *will* and *shall*. Give examples incidentally, when suitable situations present themselves. Here are possible ways:

Perhaps you occasionally take pupils on excursions, or take a football team to an 'away' match. Talk about the arrangements.

You'll ‾need to be at the bus station at nine o'˅clock. And you'll need to bring some ˅food with you.

Or when examinations are near:

If you want to pass the exami⁄nation, Tom, | you'll need to ˅work harder.

Or at the end of term:

We've been working ‾very ˅hard, this term, | ˅haven't we? We ‾all need a ˅holiday. We ‾all need to go to the ˅seaside (the ˅mountains, *etc.*).[1]

Or perhaps about your clothes or other personal possessions (or those of your pupils if this will not give offence):

‾Look at my ˅hat (˅coat, *etc.*). It's very ˅old, | ˅isn't it? I need a ˅new one. I need to go to the ˅shops | and buy a ˅new one.

A good teacher will easily think of other (and probably better) situations in which to use teaching items of this sort, items that do not fit into drills, but which are best taught and learnt by frequent use.

§ 81. *Ought* is another verb which indicates obligation. *Ought* often indicates what is morally desirable, and *ought not* what is morally undesirable. *Ought* and *ought not* are also used when giving advice on what is desirable or undesirable because of the probable results. With *ought* formal drills are again unsatisfactory. Wait until examples occur in reading-texts. Explain them in the mother tongue.

[1] Or wherever your pupils do go, if they are fortunate enough to have holidays away from home.

Then, whenever the opportunity arises, use *ought (not)* in class (and out of class, too, if you can). Here are possible ways:

When a pupil comes to class looking tired or sleepy:

⁻What time did you go to ⌄bed last night, Susan?

If the answer is a late hour:

That was very ⌄late, | ⌄wasn't it? You ought to go to bed ⌄earlier. *Or* You ⁻oughtn't to stay up so ⌄late.

When some kinds of fruit are not yet in season, but are perhaps being eaten unripe:

⁻Are there any ⌁apples (⌁mangoes, ⌁figs, *etc.*) in the shops yet? ⌄No, | they're not ⌄ripe yet, | ⌄are they? ⁻Do you ever eat ⌁unripe apples (*etc.*)? Unripe apples aren't ⌄good to eat. You ⁻oughtn't to ⌄eat them.

There are usually pupils to whom you may say:

You're not ⌄working very hard, Mary. You ought to work ⌄harder, | ⌄oughtn't you?

§ 82. *Should* is another verb used to indicate what is desirable. You may, at a later stage, use it in the situations suggested above for *ought to.*

You should go to bed ⌄earlier, *etc.*

Should is often used to make a recommendation or to give advice. It is not so strong in meaning as *ought*. The difference between *should* and *must* also deserves attention. If pupils drop litter on the classroom floor or in the school grounds, or in other ways misbehave, you may use *mustn't.*[1]

You ⁻mustn't leave bits of ⌄paper lying about on the floor (in the school playground, *etc.*).

---

[1] *Mustn't* indicates prohibition and is dealt with more fully in § 126 below. Here it is used incidentally.

You ⁻mustn't arrive ⟍late.

You ⁻mustn't ⟍talk while you're doing your exercises.

You ⁻mustn't make a ⟍noise while I'm writing on the blackboard. (*etc., etc.*)

For occasions when less severe warnings are necessary use *should*.

⟍Now, boys, | you ⁻shouldn't ⟍laugh at (Tom) when he makes a mistake.

You've made ⁻two ⟍spelling mistakes, Susan. You should be ⁻more ⟍careful.

THE CONJUNCTIONS
WHEN, BEFORE, AFTER
THE PAST AND
FUTURE PERFECT TENSES

§ **83.** The conjunction *when* is probably known.[1] *Before* and *after* are probably known in prepositional uses but not as conjunctions.[2] These three words, used as conjunctions, are essential in the presentation of the Past Perfect Tense. Before using them for this purpose, however, it is useful to present them in sequences with tenses that are already familiar. Suggestions for doing this follow.

§ **84.** Start with examples of what is habitual.

¯When do we ˻eat? We eat when we're ˅hungry. ¯When do we ˻drink? We drink when we're ˅thirsty. ¯When do we go to ˻bed? We go to bed when we're ˅tired.[3]

Put questions to the class.

¯When do you ˻eat, Paul? (I eat when I'm ˅hungry.) ¯Do you ever eat when you're ⁄not hungry, Tom? (˻No, | I ˅don't, *or* ˻Yes, | sometimes I ˅do.) ¯When do we ˻drink, Harry? (We drink when we're ˅thirsty.) (*etc., etc.*)

Continue with statements about everyday activities:

I get up every morning at ¯half-past ˅six. ¯What do I do

---

[1] See *Stage Two*, Chapter Twenty-five.

[2] See *Stage One*, § 174.

[3] If *to be tired* is a new teaching item, give the equivalent in the language of your pupils. Do not confuse your pupils by saying that it is a passive construction.

after I get ⌄up? I ⌄wash myself. I put my ⌄clothes on. I have ⌄breakfast. I put my clothes on ‾after I have ⌄washed myself. I have breakfast ‾after I have put my ⌄clothes on. I ‾always wash myself before I have ⌄breakfast. I ‾always wash my hands before I have ⌄dinner, | and ⌄supper.

§ 85. If your pupils have had, in their textbooks, examples of how letters are written in English, the following sequence may be used.

‾What do you do ⌄first, | when you write a ⌄letter? You write your ad⌄dress, | ⌄don't you? ‾Where do you ⌄write the address, Paul? (I write it in the ‾top right-hand ⌄corner.[1]) ‾What do you do ⌄next? ‾What do you do when you've written the ad⌄dress? You write the ⌄date, | ⌄don't you? ‾After you've written your ad⌃dress, | you write the ⌄date. ‾Where do you write the ⌄date, Tom? (I write it ‾under the ad⌄dress.)

‾What do you do when you've ⌄written the letter? You put it in an ⌄envelope. ‾What do you put on the ⌄envelope, | before you ⌄post it? You put a ⌄stamp on the envelope.

This sequence gives practice in the Simple Present and the Present Perfect Tenses and also illustrates the conjunctions *when, after,* and *before.* Give repetitions, and then require answers. Ask for long and complete answers, so that pupils use the clauses in their answers.

§ 86. Next use sequences in which the Future Tense occurs in the main clause and the Simple Present in the subordinate clauses. Give numerous repetitions before you require pupils to answer questions or to make statements.

[1] See *Stage Two*, § 124. If such phrases as *top (bottom), right- (left-) hand corner* are not known, it is a simple matter to teach them.

⁻Will you[1] come to school to∕morrow (*or* next ∕Monday, *etc.*)? ∖Yes, | you ∖will. ⁻Will you have a lesson from ∕me? (∖Yes, | we ∖will.) ⁻When you come to school to∕morrow, | you'll have a ⁻lesson from ∖me, | ∖won't you?

This is a convenient opportunity for the presentation of the Present Progressive Tense indicating future plans. You may say:

I'm going to (∖X)[2] next week (*or* month). ⁻When I go to (∕X), | I shall see my ∖brother (*or* ∖father, ∖sister, *etc.*). *Or* ⁻When I go to (∕X), I shall visit the mu∖seum (the uni∖versity, *etc.*). *Or* I shall perhaps see the ∖President (the Prime ∖Minister, *etc.*).[3]

I'm going to the ⁻sea∖side (the ∖mountains, *etc.*) on Sunday. When I ∕get there, | I shall have a ∖swim (have a ∖walk, *etc.*).

You may talk about the textbook, and recall the use of *still*.[4] Hold the textbook up.

⁻How many pages of this book have we ∖read now? (We've read ∖eighty pages.) ⁻How many pages have we ∖still to read? (We ⁻still have ∖twenty pages to read.) ⁻When we've finished ∕this book, | we shall start reading Book ∖Four.)

Your daily routine after school will provide further sequences.

⁻When I get ∕home this afternoon, | after ∕school, | I shall have a cup of ∖tea. When (*or* After) I've had my ∕tea, | I shall perhaps read a ∖book (go for a ∖walk, *etc.*). At

---

[1] Or *shall you* if this is what your syllabus or textbooks require you to use.

[2] Give the name of a place known to your pupils.

[3] Complete the sentence in any way you wish, provided that it is within the vocabulary range of your pupils.

[4] As presented in *Stage Two*, Chapter Fourteen.

seven o'⟋clock, | I shall have my ⟍supper. When (*or* After)
I've had my ⟋supper, | I shall listen to the ⟍radio. (*etc., etc.*)

As indicated here, you may use either *when* or *after* in the last
sequences.

§ 87. The next step is to put questions for answers from the class.
You may repeat the sequences about writing and posting a letter.
Ask for long answers so that pupils use the conjunctions in their
answers.

⏋What do you do when (*or* after) you've written the
ad⟍dress? (After I've written the ad⟋dress, | I write the
⟍date.) Do you post the letter without a ⟋stamp on the
envelope, | or do you post it ⟍after you've put a stamp on
it? (I post it ⟍after I've put a stamp on it.)

You may ask questions about what your pupils do after school.

⏋What do you ⟍do, Paul, | when you get home from
⟍school? (I have a cup of ⟍tea, | play with my ⟍brothers,
do my ⟍homework, | listen to the ⟍radio, *etc.*)

Many different answers are possible to questions of this sort, of
course, and there may be hesitation in giving them. If so, help pupils
by putting questions until you get the answer 'Yes'.

⏋Do you play with your ⟋brothers? (⟍No, | I ⟍don't.)
Do you listen to the ⟋radio? (⟍Yes, | I ⟍do.) ⏋What do ⟍you
do, | when you get home from ⟍school, Tom? ⟍Long
answer, please. (When I get home from ⟋school, | I ⏋listen
to the ⟍radio.)

⏋What will you do when the ⟍holidays come, Mary?
⏋Will you go to the sea⟋side? (⟍No, | I ⟍won't.) ⏋Will you
go to (⟋X)? (⟍Yes, | I ⟍will.) ⏋What will you ⟍do, Mary, |

when the ꜜholidays come? ꜜLong answer, please. (When the ꜛholidays come, | I'll go to ꜜX.)

⁻What will you do after you have ꜜsupper this evening, Elsie? Will you read a ꜛbook? (ꜜNo, | I ꜜwon't read a book. I'll listen to the ꜜradio.) ⁻What will ꜜyou do after you have supper, Betty? ꜜLong answer, please. (After I have ꜛsupper, | I'll play with my ꜜsister.)

When there are numerous possible answers, as here, patience is needed to get the kind of answer you want for drilling the teaching item with which you are concerned, here the use of the Future Tense in the main clause. Your knowledge of the habits of your pupils will help. The sequences supplied here can be taken as a model for procedure, but the choice of activities, *etc.*, is for you to make.

§ **88.** When pupils use these conjunctions confidently with the tenses illustrated above, you may present the Past Perfect Tense. The Past Perfect requires care in the choice of situations. It is used to indicate the earlier of two events in past time. In many cases, however, the sequence of past events is clear without the use of the Past Perfect. Each of a number of past events may be described by the use of the Simple Past. For examples:

I woke up at ⁻six o'ꜜclock this morning. I got out of ꜜbed, | cleaned my ꜜteeth, | ꜜwashed myself, | put my ꜜclothes on, | had my ꜜbreakfast, | and came to ꜜschool.

The Past Perfect is used only when it is needed to make clear that two past events were separated in time.

Here are sequences that may be used. The pronoun 'I' may be replaced by 'Mr X', 'Miss Y', 'My brother', 'My friend Z', if you prefer not to make statements about yourself, and instead of 'the cinema', 'a football match', *etc.*, you may prefer other social activities, *etc.*, that are usual in your town or district.

Start by making two simple statements.

I went to the ꜜcinema (a ꜜconcert, a ꜜfootball match,

etc.) yesterday (*or* on Saturday, *or* one day last week).
The cinema (concert, *etc*.) started at ⁻two o'ↄclock. I got
there at ⁻ten minutes ↄpast two. I was ↄlate, | ↄwasn't I?
I was ⁻ten minutes ↄlate.

These statements have clearly established the difference in time
which is so important. Now use *when* and the Past Perfect.

When I got to the ↗cinema, | the film had al⁻ready
ↄstarted. (When I got to the ↗football ground, | the match
had al⁻ready ↄstarted, *etc*.)

Another sequence:

My friend Y wanted to go to ↄX last week. The train
for X leaves at ⁻half past ↄtwo. My friend was ↄlate. He
got to the station at ⁻twenty to ↄthree. When he got to
the ↗station, | the train had al⁻ready ↄleft.[1]

If you have a class of girls, the following sequence may be used.
Adapt the wording to fit whatever method of heating is usual in your
town ('light the gas', 'turn on the current', *etc*.).

My wife (My servant, Mrs Y, *etc*.) wanted to ⁻make
some ↄcoffee yesterday. First she made a ↄfire. When she
had made a ↗fire, | she ⁻boiled some ↄwater. When she
had boiled the ↗water, | she ⁻poured it on to the ↄcoffee, | in
the ↄcoffee-pot.

Repeat the sequence using *after* instead of *when*, and perhaps
using 'cook some rice', or 'bake some bread', instead of 'make some
coffee'. (Talk about cooking activities that are usual in your country
and do not introduce more than two or three new 'content words'.)

§ 89. When you have given numerous sequences, with as many
repetitions as you think necessary, put questions to the class.

[1] At this point you may add 'He missed the train' if you think this use of
miss is worth teaching.

⁻When you got to ↘school this morning, Tom, | ⁻had the lessons already ↗started? ↘Long answer, please. (↘No, | ⁻when I got to ↗school this morning, | the lessons ⁻hadn't ↘started yet.)

⁻When you got ↘home yesterday afternoon, Paul, | ⁻had your father got back from ↗work? (↘No, | when I got ↗home yesterday, | my father ↘hadn't got back from work. *Or* ↘Yes, | when I got ↗home yesterday, | my father had al⁻ready got back from ↘work.)

If you know that pupils have recently attended a football match, or other similar event, use these questions:

⁻Did you go to the ↗football match (school ↗sports, *etc.*) last week (last Saturday, *etc.*), James? (↘Yes, | I ↘did.) ⁻What time did the match ↘start? (It started at ⁻three o'↘clock.) ⁻Did you get to the football ground be↗fore | or ↘after the match had started? (I got to the ground be↘fore the match had started.)

Other questions may be made from the sequences you yourself used (as in § 85 above).

⁻What did you ↘do, John, | ⁻after you had had ↘supper yesterday evening? ↘Long answer, please. (After I had had ↗supper, | I read a ↘book.)

§ 90. The further use of *before* and the Past Perfect Tense may be dealt with after an interval of a few weeks or months. The situations already used may be used again.

My friend Y wanted to go to ↘X last week. The train for X leaves at ⁻six o'↘clock. My friend got to the station at ⁻ten ↘past six. When he got to the ↗station, | the train had ↘left. The train had left be↘fore he got to the station.

Similarly, in other sequences:

I got to the football ground ˅early. I got there be‾fore
the match had ˅started.

I got to school ˅early this morning. I got here be‾fore
the bell had rung for the first ˅lesson. (*etc.*, *etc.*)

§ 91. The oral work on the Past Perfect should be followed by
written exercises. Your textbook probably has suitable exercises.
If not, you may prepare suitable exercises yourself. Here are
specimens of various types:

(i) Pairs of sentences to be combined by the use of *when* or *after*.
   He counted his money. Then he put it away carefully.
   (When he *had counted* his money, he put it away carefully.)
   He washed himself. Then he put his clothes on.
   (When he *had washed* himself, he . . .)
   Mary did her homework. Then she went out to play.
   (When Mary *had done* her homework, she . . .)

(ii) Sentences to be recomposed with *before* instead of *when*.
   When we reached the football ground, the game *had not
   started*.
   (We reached the football ground before the game *had
   started*.)
   When the bell rang, we *had not finished* the exercise.
   (The bell rang before we *had finished* the exercise.)
   When Tom came to my house, I *had not had* my supper.
   (Tom came to my house before I *had had* my supper.)
      Note that in this type, the main clause is to be changed
   from negative to affirmative.

(iii) Sentences in which an infinitive in parentheses is to be replaced
   by a Past Perfect Tense:
   When Susan got to school, the first lesson (*start*) already.
   (*had already started*)
   The train (*leave*) when we reached the station. (*had left*)

If you compose exercises of this kind it is a wise precaution to
check the answers yourself before you write the sentences on the
blackboard or duplicate them. It is also necessary to see that they

do not include structures and items of vocabulary not yet learnt by your pupils.

§ **92.** The Past Perfect Tense is also used in reported speech (e.g. after *said* and *told*). It may replace the Simple Past and the Present Perfect. A change of Tense is not necessary in all cases, so care is needed when you give examples. If you ask the question, 'Have you seen the film at the X cinema, John?' and receive the answer 'Yes', you may say: 'John said that he has seen the film', with the Present Perfect unchanged in the reported speech. If the answer is, 'Yes, I saw it yesterday', you may say, 'John answered that he saw it yesterday', with the Past Tense unchanged in the reported speech.

The change to Past Perfect is needed only when the difference in time is not clearly indicated without it.

John told me on Tuesday that he had been to the cinema the day before.

(Direct speech: John said to me on Tuesday, 'I went to the cinema yesterday'.)

The use of the Past Perfect in reported speech is not a suitable item for oral drills. There are too many possible complications. Postpone it, therefore, until you are required by your Syllabus or textbooks to deal with the problems of reported speech.[1]

§ **93.** The Future Perfect Tense is not of high frequency. When examples occur in your textbooks you may spend a few minutes on an oral presentation. Do so with the preposition *by* and with examples in the Present and Past Perfect.[2]

˘How many pages of this book have we ˅read now? We've read ˅fifty pages, | ˅haven't we? ˘How many pages had we read by the end of last ˅week? We'd read forty- ˅four pages. ˘How many pages shall (*or* will) we have read by the end of ˅next week? Perhaps we shall have read fifty- ˅five pages.

[1] This is a subject which is given exaggerated importance in some countries, probably because it is possible to give numerous 'rules', and because it is liked by examiners.

[2] This is probably a new use of *by*, so explain it if necessary.

Give another sequence using the number of years your pupils have been in the school.

¯How many years have you been in this ↘school now? ¯How many years will you have been here by nineteen-sixty-↘eight?[1]

Use the blackboard for further examples. Write the names of a man, a town, and a year, for example, *Mr Green, Madras, 1950.* Then make statements and ask questions.

Mr Green ¯went to live in Madras in nineteen-↘fifty. He's ¯still ↘living there. ¯How long had he been living there in nineteen-fifty-↘five? He'd been living there for ¯five ↘years. ¯How long has he been living there ↘now? He's been living there for ↘ . . . years. ¯How long will he have been living there in nineteen-↘seventy, | if he doesn't ↘leave Madras? He'll have been living there for ↘twenty years.

Write another name, another town, and a different year, and put questions to the class. It is unnecessary to give many examples of this Tense. Note that you have used the Future Perfect Progressive in these last examples. This should not be a problem to your pupils. They have used the progressive forms of other tenses.[2]

[1] Give any suitable future year.

[2] See *Stage Two*, § 214.

CHAPTER ELEVEN (§§ 94–106)

MORE CONJUNCTIONS
BECAUSE, AS, SINCE, SO; WHILE, AS; ALTHOUGH, BUT; SINCE (for time); *TILL, UNTIL*

§ 94. It is not possible to predict when the conjunctions listed above will occur in reading material. Their places in Syllabuses vary considerably. In this chapter suggestions are made for presenting them and procedures are given. The material supplied here should not be presented in sequence, as a whole. It may be used when these words occur for the first time.

§ 95. *Because* is likely to occur early in any English course. It was dealt with in *Stage Two* of these books.[1] It was used in the presentation of *could.*[2] Recall and practise this already familiar material and then present *as*.

The conjunction *as* is used to introduce a clause expressing reason. It is not used in the way that *because* is used. Compare these two statements:

(i) Tom was absent because he was ill.

(ii) As Tom was ill, he didn't come to school.

In (i) the emphasis is on the reason for Tom's absence, and the clause indicating this reason comes last. In (ii) the emphasis is on the result of Tom's illness; the clause indicating the reason comes first.

The conjunction *since* may be used in this way, too, and *since*-clauses indicating reason usually (but not always) come first.

To present *as* and *since* with this meaning, start with *because* and then make your statements with *as* or *since*. Talk about a pupil who is absent (or has recently been absent) because of illness.

¯Why was Elsie absent (*or* away) from ↘school yesterday

[1] See § 78.

[2] See § 43 of this book.

(*or* last week, *etc.*)? She was absent because she was ⅃ill
(*or* not ⅃well). ⁻As she was ⁄ill, | she ⁻didn't (*or* ⁻couldn't)
come to ⅃school.

Here are other sequences:

I was very ⅃tired yesterday evening. I went to ⅃bed early.
⁻Why did I go to ⅃bed early? Because I was ⅃tired. As I was
⁄tired, | I went to ⅃bed early.

After repetitions you may think it useful to point out to your
pupils the different positions of clauses introduced by *because* and
as. Comment should follow, not precede, examples.

§ 96. It is not practicable to ask questions for answers that
include a clause introduced by *as*. A question with *why* is normally
answered with a statement that includes *because*. So instead of the
usual question and answer drills, you may ask questions like those
given below, and then make comments (beginning with *as*) on the
answers. The questions are designed to recall and revise teaching
items recently dealt with.

⅃Paul, | are ⁻you tall enough to touch the ⁄ceiling?
(⅃No, | I'm ⅃not.) ⁻As you're not tall enough to touch the
⁄ceiling, | you'd have to stand on a ⅃chair if you wanted
to touch it, | ⅃wouldn't you?[1]
Have ⁻you (*or* Has your ⁻father) enough money to buy
a ⁄motor-car? (⅃No, | I ⅃haven't, *or* he ⅃hasn't.) ⁻As you
haven't (*or* he hasn't) enough money to buy a ⁄motor-car, |
you (*or* he) won't be able to ⅃buy one, | ⅃will you (*or* he)?[2]

If the weather is very wet, or very hot:

[1] This recalls the use of *would* (as in § 67 of this book, and *have to* (as in
§§ 72–75) of this book.

[2] This recalls the use of *be able to* (as in §§ 45–46 of this book). You may
need to explain the meaning of *enough money*.

Do ⁻you like playing tennis when it's ⌒raining (very ⌒hot), Susan? (↘No, | I ↘don't.) As it's raining (very hot) ⌒now, | you ⁻won't want to play tennis after ↘school, | ↘will you?

When some kinds of fruit are not on sale in the shops:

⁻Are there any ⌒oranges (⌒apples, ⌒mangoes) in the shops now? (↘No, | there ↘aren't.) As there are no (⌒oranges) in the shops, | we have to eat (↘mangoes).

Half a dozen sequences of this kind will help your pupils to form the association between the front-position of the clause and the greater emphasis on the result.

When *since* occurs (to introduce a clause indicating reason), repeat these sequences, and use two or three new ones.

I'd like to go to (↘London). But I'm not a rich ↘man. Since I haven't much ⌒money, | I shan't be ↘able to go to London.

§ **97.** The conjunction *so* introduces a clause indicating result. This use of *so* may be linked with the use of *as* in the preceding sections. It is again impracticable to ask questions for answers that will include a clause introduced by *so*. You can, however, use sequences to illustrate the use of the word.

You may talk about goods (e.g. fruit) that are very expensive, perhaps because they are scarce, or out of season. Choose goods and articles that are suitable for the contexts.

I wanted to buy some ↘mangoes (↘eggs, *etc.*) yesterday. They cost a ⁻lot of ↘money,[1] | so I didn't ↘buy any. *Or*, so I bought some ↘oranges. They're ↘cheap now, | ↘aren't they?

You may talk about out-of-school activities.

[1] Or, better, give the actual price.

I wanted to go for a ˅walk on Sunday. It was ˅raining hard (*or* very ˅hot), | so I ˅didn't go for a walk. I stayed at ˅home.

You may think it useful to compare *as* and *so* by writing two sentences on the blackboard:

As it was ⟋raining hard, | I ˅didn't go for a walk.
It was ˅raining hard, | so I ˅didn't go for a walk.

(There is no need to write the tone symbols on the blackboard. They are given here so that when you read the sentences aloud you may do so with a natural intonation.)

§ **98.** Your pupils have probably used the conjunction *while*.[1] It usually occurs in procedures for teaching the Past Continuous Tense. *As* may be used in some (but not all) of the contexts in which *while* is used.

Do not confuse pupils by presenting this use of *as* (for *while*) together with the use of *as* (to indicate cause or reason) dealt with in §§ 95–96 above. Deal with it only when it first occurs in reading-texts. Start with *while* and continue with *as*.

⁻While I was coming to ⟋school this morning, | I saw Mr ˅X. He was getting off a ˅bus. I saw him ⁻as he was getting off the ˅bus.

The difference between *while* and *as* is one that may perhaps be made clear by the use of the equivalent words in the language of your pupils (if, of course, two different words exist). In the sequence above *while* means 'during the time when'; *as* means 'at the moment when'.

Here is another example:

⁻Have you ever climbed a high ⟋mountain? My friend ˅X once climbed a mountain. As he climbed ⟋higher, | he got ⁻very ˅tired.

[1] See *Stage Two*, §§ 153–154.

In this example *as* means 'during the time in which', not 'at the time when'. When examples occur in reading-texts make clear to your pupils the meaning of *as* in the particular contexts.

§ **99**. *Although* may be linked with *but*. Start with simple examples of *but*, indicating contrast.

ˉLook at these two ˅books. The red book is ˅new, | but the ˉgreen book is ˅old.

ˉLook at ˅these two books. The black book is on the ˅table, | but the yellow book is on Paul's ˅desk.

You're all ˅sitting, | but I'm ˅standing. (*etc., etc.*)

Continue with other examples which can, later, be recomposed with *although*, indicating concession.

Tom worked very ˅hard, | but he ˉdidn't pass the examiˍnation.

Alˉthough Tom worked very ˄hard, | he ˉdidn't pass the examiˍnation.

It was ˅raining on Sunday, | but I ˉdidn't stay at ˅home. I went for a ˅walk.

Alˉthough it was ˄raining on Sunday, | I ˉdidn't stay at ˅home. I didn't stay at ˄home, | alˍthough it was raining on Sunday.

§ **100**. Question and answer drills are not possible for this item. Instead you may use conversion exercises. If your textbook does not include such exercises, you may make your own. Here are examples:

Mr X has a car, but he often travels by bus and by tram.

Mr Y is a rich man, but he made his money honestly.

Mr Z is nearly 90, but he is still able to see and hear well.

Require pupils to rewrite these sentences using *although*. Tell them to put *although* first:

Although Mr X has a car, he often . . .

Then tell them to put the clause at the end:

Mr X often travels by bus and by tram, although he has a car.

§ **101.** The presentation of *since* in clauses of time requires care. It provides further practice in the use of the Present Perfect Tense (both simple and progressive). Its use with a point of time (as in 'since yesterday', 'since 1958') is probably familiar to your pupils.[1] Revise this, and the use of *for* with a period of time (as in 'for three years'). You may talk about the year in which your pupils first entered the school, the year in which they started to learn English (if this is different), the number of years they have been in the school. In the sequence that follows substitute the actual year(s) and figures for those supplied.

⁻When did you first ⸌come to this school? (*or* ⸌enter this school?) You first came here in ⁻nineteen-fifty-⸌six. You've been in this school for ⁻five ⸌years. You've been here since ⁻nineteen-fifty-⸌six.

⁻When did you start learning ⸌English? You started in ⁻nineteen-fifty-⸌eight, | ⸌didn't you? You've been learning English for ⁻three ⸌years.

If further revision is needed, use the material in *Stage Two*, § 213.

§ **102.** When answers show that pupils are confident in their use of these items, present the conjunction *since*.

⁻Since you began to learn ⸍English, | three years a⸍go, | you've learnt a ⁻large number of English ⸌words, | ⸌haven't you? You've learnt to ⸌speak English. You've learnt to ⸌read English. You've learnt to ⸌write English.

Note the use of the Past Tense in the subordinate clause and the use of the Present Perfect in the main clause.

Give other sequences, using situations that are connected with your own work and out-of-school activities and those of your pupils. You may be able to adapt some of the following sequences.

[1] See *Stage Two*, §§ 213–215.

Two ╱years ago, | I went to (╲Delhi).[1] ‾Since I went to (Delhi) two ╱years ago (*or* in nineteen-╱sixty), | I've ‾not left this ╲country.

A few ╱weeks ago, | I went to the ╲cinema. I saw (╲. . .).[2] Since I saw that ╱film, | I ‾haven't ╲visited the cinema (*or* ‾haven't ╲been to the cinema).[3]

‾When did our football team play ╲X[4]? It was ‾five ╲weeks ago, | ╲wasn't it? ‾Did our team ╱win | or ╲lose, Paul? (It ╲won.) ‾Since our team won that ╱match, | ‾have we won all the ╱other matches? ╲Yes, | we ╲have. *Or* ╲No, | we ╲haven't. We've won ╱three, | and ‾lost ╲one.

§ 103. If you have difficulty in using real situations of this kind, or if the vocabulary items are unknown, you may use the sequences suggested below, less interesting probably, but perhaps easier for your pupils. Write on the blackboard:

First World War: 1914–1919
Second World War: 1939–1946

Then make statements, with questions and answers.

The First World War ‾ended in nineteen-nine╲teen. Since that war ╱ended, | there has been a╲nother World War, | ╲hasn't there? ‾When did the ╲Second World War end, Paul? (It ended in ‾nineteen-forty-╲six.) Since the ╱Second World War ended, | there have been ╲other wars.

You may talk about flying. Write the name *Lindbergh*[5] on the blackboard, and 1927.

[1] Give the name of any place abroad that you have visited.

[2] Give the name of a film that was being shown then.

[3] For this use of *been*, see *Stage Two*, § 160. If this use of *been* is not known, either avoid it or explain it.

[4] Give the name of a rival team.

[5] Pronounced /'lindbə:g/.

⁻Who was the first man to fly aˇlone, | across the Atˇlantic? ˇLindbergh was. He flew from ⁻New York to ˇParis, | in ⁻nineteen-twenty-ˇseven.

Since Lindbergh flew across the Atˊlantic, | in nineteen-twenty-ˊseven, | many ˇother persons have flown across the Atlantic. Airliners fly across the Atlantic ⁻every ˇday.

§ **104.** The next step is to ask questions to be answered by pupils. First require short answers only, and then long answers including the *since*-clause. Use questions with vocabulary items which are well known. Questions about the textbook may be used.

⁻When did we start reading this ˇbook, Tom? (We started reading it in Sepˇtember.) ⁻How many pages (*or* lessons) have we ˇread, | since we ⁻started reading it in Sepˇtember? (We've read ˇforty pages.) Now the ˇlong answer, Tom. (We've read ˇforty pages, | since we started reading it in Sepˇtember.)

Long answers are required so that pupils may themselves use the *since*-clauses. But for this kind of drill written exercises are more convenient than oral drills. Your textbooks, if well designed, will include exercises in which infinitive forms (in parentheses) are to be replaced by the correct tense forms. Here are examples:
Since Mary (leave) school two years ago, she (work) in an office.
    The answers are *left, has been working.*
Since we (come) to this school in 1957, we (learn) a lot of English.
    The answers are *came, have learnt.*

§ **105.** When your pupils are familiar with the tense sequences illustrated above (Past Tense and Present Perfect), give a few examples in which the Present Perfect is used in both clauses. (It is unwise to make rules or general statements about tense sequences. Examples are always better than rules.)

⁻Since you've been in this ˊschool, | you've learnt ˇmany things, | ˇhaven't you?

Compare the Past Tense and the Present Perfect in the *since-*clause:

⁻Since I began to ⸍teach you (*or* ⁻Since I've been giving you ⸍lessons), | I've learnt your ⸜names, | ⸜haven't I? I know you all by ⸜name now.

§ 106. *Till* and *until* are probably known as prepositions, in such phrases as 'from three o'clock till five o'clock'.[1] Their use as conjunctions is not difficult and will not need numerous examples. As *until* introduces clauses of time, its use may be compared with that of *when*.

This lesson will end when the ⸜bell rings. We shall stop when the ⸜bell rings.

In these sentences the Simple Present is used in the clause. The same is true of a clause with *until* for future time.

We shall continue our lesson until the ⸜bell rings. When the ⸍bell rings, | we shall ⸜stop.

When, at the end of the lesson, the bell has rung, you may say:

⁻Did we stop be⸍fore the bell rang? ⸜No, | we ⸜didn't. We ⁻waited until the ⸜bell rang.

Other examples will occur in reading-texts. You may call attention to the tense sequences in these.

---

[1] See *Stage Two*, §§ 151–152.

CHAPTER TWELVE (§§ 107–116)

THE PASSIVE VOICE

§ 107. If you have followed the order in which teaching items are presented in these books, or even if you have presented most of them in a different order, your pupils will be familiar with a small number of examples of construction in the passive voice. They will know 'to be made of', 'to be called', and 'to be used for'.[1]

If the passive voice is taught through grammatical rules there is the danger that pupils (and even some teachers) may produce sentences that are unlikely ever to be heard or seen outside the classroom. To convert 'I ate a good breakfast' to 'A good breakfast was eaten by me' may illustrate rules, but it is a wrong and harmful procedure. It results in artificial English.

§ 108. One procedure which requires no grammatical explanation is the use of sentences in which a past participle is used in the same way as an adjective. There is no need to present the sentences re-composed in the active voice. Here are specimen sequences. They include revision of other teaching items.

¯Look at this ↘box. It's ↘large (*or* ↘small, ↘light, ↘heavy, *etc.*), | ↘isn't it? It's made of ↘wood. It's ↘locked.[2] Here's the ↘key. ¯Is the box ↗still locked? ↘No, | it ↘isn't. I can ↘open it now. ↘Look, | I'm ¯turning the ↘key. The box is ↘locked now. I'm turning the key a↘gain. Now the box ↘isn't locked.

For the present do not use such statements as 'I'm locking the box', 'I've locked the box'.

Next hold up something that is obviously broken, perhaps an old wooden ruler, a cup or drinking glass, a pencil with a broken point,

[1] See *Stage One*, § 118, and *Stage Two*, § 119.

[2] Make the meaning clear by showing that the box cannot be opened.

whatever is available (but not a piece of chalk, because its small size might be the result of use).

ˉLook at this ⌄ruler. It's not a very ⌄good one, | ⌄is it? It's ⌄broken.

ˉLook at this ⌄pencil. I'm trying to ⌄write with it, | but I ⌄can't. The ⌄point's broken. This pencil has a ˉbroken ⌄point.

Perhaps you can provide an old watch that no longer goes.

ˉLook at this ⌄watch. ˉWhat ⌄time is it by this watch, Paul? (It's ˉsix o'⌄clock.) ˉIs that the ⌄right time, Paul? (⌄No, | it ⌄isn't.) ˉWhat's the ⌄right time, John? (It's . . .) This watch isn't ⌄going.[1] It's ⌄broken.

ˉLook at that ⌄window. Is ˉthat window ⌄broken? ⌄No, | it ⌄isn't. ˉAre ⌄any of the windows in this room broken? ⌄No, | ⌄none of them are broken.[2]

§ 109. If your pupils know the words *fur*, *hair* and *feathers*, use *covered*.

ˉWhat's a ⌄cat covered with? It's covered with ⌄fur. ˉWhat's a ⌄dog covered with? It's covered with ⌄hair. ˉWhat are ⌄birds covered with? They're covered with ⌄feathers.

If the conditions of the roads in your part of the country justify the statements:

ˉWhat are the ⌄roads covered with, | when it hasn't ⌄rained for a long time? They're covered with ⌄dust.

---

[1] Ask a pupil to translate this sentence as a test of comprehension.

[2] For *none* see *Stage Two*, Chapter Three. If you have not used this word much, you may need to recall it. Tell your class that *none* may mean either 'not one' or 'not any' and may, according to context, be used with the singular or plural form of a verb.

ˉWhat are they covered with after it has ˅rained? They're covered with ˅mud. ˉLook at my ˅fingers. They're covered with ˅chalk dust.

If your pupils know the words *province*, *county*, *prefecture*, or other words used for divisions of a country:

Pakistan is divided into ˅provinces. Japan is divided into ˅prefectures. ˉHow is Great ˅Britain divided? It's divided into ˅counties. How is ˅India divided? It's divided into ˅States. Madras is a ˉState in ˅India. Madras is the name of a ˅town, | ˅too, | ˅isn't it?

§ 110. You will select from the examples suggested above those that are best fitted to your pupils' knowledge (of vocabulary, geography, *etc.*), and to local conditions. The aim of this presentation is to familiarize your pupils with the passive construction (*is* or *are* and a past participle) in the simplest form (without the use of *by* and the agent). When this aim has been accomplished, you may use some of your examples again, this time with examples of the active voice. Here are some procedures:

ˉLook at this ˅box. It's ˅open, | ˅isn't it? I'm going to ˅close it. I'm going to ˉput the ˅lid down. I've ˉclosed the ˅box. ˉWhat have I just ˅done, Susan? (You've ˉclosed the ˅box.) ˅Yes, | the box is ˅closed now. ˉIs it ⁄locked, Mary? (˅No, | it ˅isn't locked.) I'm going to ˅lock it. I've ˉturned the ˅key. ˉIs the box ⁄locked now, Edith? ˅Long answer, please. (˅Yes, | the box is ˅locked now.) ˉWho ˅locked the box, Janet? Did ⁄I lock it, | or did ˅you lock it? (˅You locked it.)

ˉLook at this ˅pencil. There's a ˉgood ˅point on it. ˉCan I ⁄write with this pencil, Sarah? (˅Yes, | you ˅can.) I'm going to ˉbreak the ˅point. I've ˉbroken the ˅point. ˉCan I write with this pencil ⁄now, Ruth? (˅No, | you

ᐸcan't.) ‾Why can't I write with the pencil ᐸnow? Because the ᐸpoint is broken.

§ 111. *Tear* is another useful verb. If it is not known, make statements to demonstrate the meaning and to give the forms *tear, tore* and *torn*.[1] Write these three words on the blackboard (after using them orally).

ᐸLook, | this is a piece of ᐸpaper. I'm going to ᐸtear it. I've ‾torn this piece of ᐸpaper. ‾What did I ᐸdo, | a few seconds aᐸgo? I ‾tore this piece of ᐸpaper.[2]

Repeat two or three times if the words are new. Then hold up not the torn piece of paper, but something different, or better, several different things, each obviously torn.

‾Look at this piece of ᐸcloth. It's ᐸtorn, | ᐸisn't it? ‾Look at this ᐸcoat. The ᐸsleeve's torn, | ᐸisn't it? It's torn at the ᐸelbow (*or* ᐸhere).[3]

You probably have an old and valueless book or magazine.

‾Look at this old ᐸbook. Some of the ᐸpages are torn, | ᐸaren't they? Some of the pages have been ‾torn ᐸout.

§ 112. Your last statement was in the Present Perfect. Do not comment on this. Instead, proceed to give further examples.

‾Look at this old book aᐸgain. ‾Several pages have been torn ᐸout. I'm going to tear out aᐸnother page.[4] ‾Come ᐸhere, Paul. ‾Tear out aᐸnother page. ‾What has Paul

---

[1] *tear* /teə*/, *tore* /to:*/, *torn* /to:n/.

[2] You could, of course, add 'in two', or 'into pieces', but this would add an extra burden. Your main aim is the passive construction.

[3] It should not be difficult to bring to class an old garment of some kind.

[4] Or 'tear another page out'. For the alternative positions of *out*, see *Stage Two*, Chapter Seventeen.

just ˅done? He's torn out aˑnother page. ˉTwo ˅more pages have been torn out now.

Now use *by* for the first time.

One was torn out by ˊme; | the other was torn out by ˅Paul.

Statements including *by* should be restricted to situations in which it is desired to name the agent. In the last pair of statements you wanted the contrast between *me* and *Paul*. This is why, with these two words, there is the change in pitch (ˊ*me* and ˅*Paul*).

§ 113. For further examples using *by* you may use titles of books, poems and plays, and their authors. Choose names likely to be quite familiar. Here the authors are British. You will probably find it better to use titles and authors from the literature of your own country.

ˉHave you read 'ˊHamlet'? It was written by ˅Shakespeare. ˉHave you read 'David ˊCopperfield'? It was written by ˅Dickens. ˉDo you know the poem called 'The ˊSwing'? It was written by ˅Stevenson.

§ 114. When you decide that the time has come for your pupils to use passive constructions, exercise great care not to let them use any that are not quite natural. The question 'By whom was the cloth torn?' will get the answer 'It was torn by (˅Paul, ˅me, *etc.*),' but outside the classroom the question is much more likely to be, 'Who tore this cloth?' You do not want to encourage the use of 'classroom English' that is artificial. Instead of asking questions it is preferable to require your pupils to repeat, after you, some of the sequences you used in your presentation of the new item, as in §§ 108 and 110 Questions may be asked about the material in § 109.

ˉWhat's a ˅cat covered with? (*etc.*)

Is ˉthis country divided into ˊcounties, | like Great ˊBritain, | or into ˅provinces (˅States, *etc.*)?

§ 115. As your pupils increase their vocabulary you will find many opportunities for illustrating the most important use of the passive construction, that is, for statements and questions when the name of the agent is unknown or unimportant. Here are examples:

Is ⁻this school ⸍new | or ⸜old? (It's ⸜new.) ⁻When was it ⸜built? It was built ⁻five ⸜years ago.

⁻Look at your ⸜textbooks, | page ⸜2 (*or* the ⁻last ⸜page).[1] ⁻Where were these books ⸜printed? ⁻Were they printed in ⸍this country | or in ⸜England?

One of your pupils may be absent because of illness, or an accident.

Bruce isn't at ⸜school today. He's ⸜ill, | ⸜very ill. (*Or* He was knocked down by a ⸜bus yesterday, | and ⸜hurt badly.) He was taken to ⸜hospital.

In these statements it is natural to use the passive construction. So when you see opportunities, give examples, incidentally, at the beginning or end of a lesson period. This is much more useful than the practice of requiring pupils to convert sentences from active to passive voice with answers that are artificial.

§ 116. One of the most typical and frequent uses of the passive in English is with such participles as *pleased, delighted, surprised, worried,* followed by an infinitive. Another typical use is in such phrases as 'I've been told (that)', 'I've been asked whether'. When your pupils have learnt the structure 'glad (sorry, pleased, surprised, *etc.*) to know (learn, *etc.*)',[2] use such phrases occasionally. You can help your pupils, at this stage, if you make occasional statements in class using these structures. Remember that examples are almost always better than 'rules'.

---

[1] We usually find, at the beginning or end of a book, the name of the printers and the town where the book was printed.

[2] See Chapter Fourteen in this book.

POSSIBILITY;
PROBABILITY AND LIKELIHOOD;
PERMISSION AND PROHIBITION

§ **117.** If you have presented the material in Chapter III of this book, your pupils will be familiar with the pattern: *It is* × adjective × *to* × infinitive. They will understand the sentence: 'It is possible to go from London to Tokyo by air'. There are other patterns for such adjectives as *possible*, *probable*, *likely* and *certain*. These are dealt with in the next section.

§ **118.** Start with *perhaps*, which you have used frequently. Then continue with *possible* (*probable*) *that*.

If you are in a country where the weather changes frequently, this provides an easy sequence.

¯Will it ⌐rain tomorrow? Perhaps it ⌐will. It's ⌐possible that it will rain tomorrow. *Or* ¯Will it be ⌐fine¹ tomorrow? Perhaps it ⌐will. It's ⌐possible that the weather will be fine.

If you are in a country where the weather is regular (e.g. with a long dry season, or a wet season), you may use *probable* or *certain* (whichever you think right).

¯Will it ⌐rain (be ⌐hot, ⌐dry) tomorrow? ⌐Yes, | it's ¯probable (¯certain) that it will ⌐rain (be ⌐hot, ⌐dry, *etc*.) tomorrow.²

---

¹ *Fine* often means (in Great Britain) 'without rain'. It does not necessarily imply sunshine.

² Compare § 33 in this book, and the use of 'It is likely (certain) to rain (be hot, *etc*.)'. Because we cannot say 'It is possible (probable) to rain', it is wiser not to use *likely* and *certain* in the construction with an infinitive in the same series as 'It is probable (certain) that . . .'.

You may, after repetitions, vary your statements by using the adverbs.

ˉWill it ⌃rain tomorrow? ⌄Yes, | it probably ⌄will.
ˉWill it be ⌃hot again tomorrow? ⌄Yes, | it certainly ⌄will.

§ 119. The use of these adjectives and adverbs is not the commonest way of indicating possibility and likelihood. There are other ways which are far more common, especially in colloquial style. The verb *may* is very often used. You may say 'It may rain (be fine, *etc.*) tomorrow', but for variety it is better to use a different situation. You may pretend that you cannot find something, and make statements about where it may be. Look for your pen, or keys, or some other article, in two or three pockets. Then say:

I can't find my ⌄pen. It isn't in ⌃this pocket. It isn't in ⌃this pocket. Perhaps it's in ⌄this pocket. ⌄No, | it isn't in ⌄this pocket. It may be on the ⌄desk, | under these ⌄papers. ⌄No, | it isn't ⌄there. Perhaps I ⌄dropped it. It may be on the ⌄floor. ˉWill you ⌃look for it, please, Tom? ˉCan you ⌃see it? It ⌄isn't on the floor. It may be in this ⌄drawer (*or* in this ⌄bag). ⌄Yes, | ⌄here it is.

This sequence gives numerous examples of the use of *may* to indicate probability. If you want your pupils to use the new word, you may use a game. Send one of the pupils out of the room. Then hide a small article (a key, a ring, a coin) and tell the class to make suggestions about its hiding-place (all incorrect, of course) when the pupil is called in and told to find the missing article. This pupil will ask questions (and get practice in using prepositions). The pupil who answers the question will say 'No', and then make a statement with *may*. The pupils do all the talking (always desirable if they are using words and structures they have mastered). You say:

There's a ⌄key in this room. Try to ⌄find it, Paul. ˉAsk ⌄questions.

The game might go in this way:

ˉIs it in your ⸝pocket, Tom? (⸜No; | it may be in ⸜John's pocket.) ˉIs it in ⸝your pocket, John? (⸜No; | it may be in that ⸜drawer.) ˉIs it in that ⸝drawer, Harry? (⸜No; | it may be on the ⸜floor, | under my ⸜desk.)

The questions may continue for two or three minutes, until at last the correct answer is given and the game ends.

§ 120. Use *may* in this meaning on any suitable occasion that arises during the next few weeks or months, so that pupils become familiar with it in other situations. If a pupil is absent (and no one knows why), you may say, 'He may be ill'. If you plan to give your class a test, say, a day or two in advance, 'I may give you a test on Wednesday'. Give an example of *may* with the perfect infinitive. Start with *perhaps* and then use *may*. For example, if a pupil is not present at the beginning of the first period in the morning:

Paul isn't ⸜here yet. Perhaps he has missed his ⸜bus. He may have missed his ⸜bus.

If you know that he cycles to school:

Perhaps he has had a ⸜puncture. He may have had a ⸜puncture.

When a new teaching item cannot easily be fitted into oral drills, it is desirable (if the item is useful and important) to use it incidentally whenever you see an opportunity.

§ 121. The use of *might* can be shown by using it in clauses. Use sentences on the blackboard.
He said, 'I may be going to London'.
He said that he might be going to London.
Might is also used with reference to future time, and in this case indicates a possibility that is more remote, less likely to be fulfilled. Perhaps lotteries are popular in your country. Unless you think it wrong to encourage this kind of gambling, you may talk in this way:

I sometimes buy a ⸜lottery ticket, | but I've ˉnever won

a ↘prize. (*Or* I won a ⁻small ↘prize last year.) I ⁻might win a ↘large prize one day.

§ 122. After your pupils have learnt to use *whether*,[1] give occasional examples of this word followed by a statement with *may*. Here are examples:

I ⁻don't ↘know whether I shall give you a test next week. I ↗may give you a test; | I may ↘not. I'll⁻tellyouto↘morrow.

I'm ⁻not ↘sure whether I shall go to X on Sunday. I ↗may go; | I may ↘not. If it ↗rains, | I shall ↘not go.

§ 123. *May* is used to indicate permission. This use is best presented by incidental use. Do not give a talk or lecture on all the uses of *may*. Your aim should be to help pupils to *use* English, not to acquire information *about* English. When a pupil has been standing at his desk (to make a series of statements, ask and answer questions, *etc.*), say to him, when he has finished:

You may sit ↘down now, Tom.

Or when he has been at the blackboard:

You may go back to your ↘seat now.

Encourage pupils to make requests to you in English. You will probably have to tell them how to do this. Teach them to use such questions as these:

⁻May I ask a ↗question, please?
⁻May I leave the ↗room for a minute, please?[2]
It's very ↘hot today. ⁻May I open the ↗window, please?

You will answer:

↘Yes, | you ↘may. (*Or* ↘No, | you may ↘not.)[3]

---

[1] See § 145 below.

[2] For example, if they want to go to the W.C.

[3] Compare *musnt't* for a prohibition, as in § 126 below.

§ **124.** Pupils can be helped to form the right associations by the use of English notices where these are suitable. If you have a library of English books (simplified texts for rapid reading, *etc.*), place a notice on or near the shelves: *Pupils may borrow not more than two books at a time. They may not keep the books for more than one week.*[1] If there are reference books on the shelves, place a notice by these: *Dictionaries must not be taken away from the Library* (or *classroom*). Such notices, seen every day, will quickly cause pupils to understand *may* and *may not*, and the difference between *may not* and *must not*.

§ **125.** When a pupil makes a request with *may*, it is a simple matter to present the past tense form *might*. A pupil says:

⁻May I open the ⁄window, please?

You say:

⁻What did Paul ⟍ask me? He asked me ⁻whether he might open the ⟍window.[2]

§ **126.** As already noted in this chapter, *must not* indicates more than the contrary of permission (for which *may not* is often enough). It is used to indicate that something is not allowed, that it is prohibited or forbidden. Suggestions for using it are given in § 82 in this book, where it is compared with *should* and *should not*, used for giving advice or friendly warnings.

If your pupils are like children in most parts of the world you will find numerous opportunities for using *mustn't*.

You ⁻mustn't ⟍copy. You ⁻mustn't ⟍shout (make a lot of ⟍noise) when I leave the room. You ⁻mustn't leave your bicycle in the school ⟍corridor, Tom. You ⁻mustn't use your dictionaries during the ⟍test. (*etc.*, *etc.*)

§ **127.** Another way of indicating prohibition is seen in such public notices as 'No parking' and 'No smoking'. These mean:

[1] Adapted to your own rules, of course.

[2] Only, of course, after *whether* has been taught.

'Cars must not be parked here', 'Smoking is not allowed here'. Your pupils may be told about these when you think the information will be useful. The 'No smoking' sign is commonly seen in airliners during take-off and landing.

CHAPTER FOURTEEN (§§ 128–136)

SOME ADJECTIVE PATTERNS
NOUNS, PARTICIPLES AND GERUNDS
(AS USED TO MODIFY NOUNS)

§ **128.** Adjectives are more easily taught and learnt than verbs. Your pupils have been using adjectives confidently. They have learnt the comparison of adjectives, including those that are irregular. They have learnt to use some adjectives with infinitives. There are other items to be presented. In this chapter some of these items are dealt with, together with the use of nouns, participles, and gerunds to modify nouns.

§ **129.** Many adjectives and participles are used with *to* and an infinitive. So far your pupils have heard and used sentences such as:[1]
This book is easy (difficult) to read.
Milk is good to drink.
They will, sooner or later, meet such sentences as these:[2]
He was glad (delighted, *etc.*) to see us.
Are you ready to start?
The child was afraid to go into the dark room.

Many of the adjectives and participles used in sentences such as these express emotion of some kind. It is not easy, therefore, to find examples that fit well into oral drills, though there will certainly be many occasions on which you may use the pattern incidentally in ordinary classroom situations. This approach is probably the best. Here are some suggestions:

When a pupil is absent through illness, or returns after being ill:

I'm ⁻sorry to tell you that Paul is ⌍ill. He's been taken to ⌍hospital.

You'll be ⁻sorry to know that Susan is ⌍ill. She'll be a⁻way from ⌍school for a few days.

[1] See § 34 of this book.
[2] See *A Guide to Patterns and Usage*, § 82b, for this pattern.

You'll be ⁻glad to know that Paul's ꜜwell again. He'll be ⁻back at school next ꜜweek.

When results of tests or examinations are to be announced:

You'll be ⁻glad to know that you've all done ꜜwell (ꜜpassed).

I'm ⁻glad (⁻happy) to tell you that most of you did ꜜwell.

You'll be ⁻sorry to know that some of you have ꜜfailed.

Later, when your pupils have a larger vocabulary, you may use past participles such as *disappointed*, *delighted*, *excited*, *surprised* when suitable situations make their use possible.

You'll be ex⁻cited (de⁻lighted) to know that next Monday will be an extra ꜜholiday.

§ 130. The adjective *afraid* is used in this pattern. Your pupils probably know two predicative adjectives already. They have probably used *awake* and *asleep*.[1] *Afraid* is not used attributively. Compare:

The boy was a⁻fraid to go there a ꜜlone.

The frightened boy ⁻wouldn't go there a ꜜlone.

Afraid is used with *of* and also with *to* and an infinitive. You may present the two patterns together.[2]

Young children are sometimes a⁻fraid to go near big ꜜdogs. They're a⁻fraid to go near big ꜜhorses. They're a⁻fraid to go into a dark ꜜroom, | at ꜜnight. (*etc.*, *etc.*)

Repeat with *of*.

Young children are sometimes a⁻fraid of big ꜜdogs. They're a⁻fraid of big ꜜhorses. They're a⁻fraid of the ꜜdark.[3]

[1] See *Stage Two*, § 101.

[2] Postpone the pattern *afraid* (*that*).

[3] Give the meaning of 'the dark' in the language of your pupils.

Use *afraid* in both these patterns in questions:

⁻What are ↗you afraid of, Tom? ⁻Are you afraid of
↗snakes? Are ⁻you afraid to cross a busy ↗street, Mary?
(*etc., etc.*)

§ 131. Another group of adjectives used with *to* and an infinitive
includes *certain, sure, likely, ready, able*, and the ordinals (*first,
second, etc.*), with *next* and *last*. Your pupils have used *certain* and
likely with *it*[1]; in such sentences as 'It is certain (likely) to be hot in
July'. They must also have examples of these adjectives, and others,
in sentences with a subject other than an infinitive phrase.
   Ready is easily demonstrated.

⁻Open your ↘notebooks. ⁻Take up your ↘pens. You're
⁻all ready to ↘write now.

Give examples in other situations.

When you've had your ↗breakfast, | you're ⁻ready to
go to ↘school. You're ⁻ready for ↘school.
   In the ↗evening, | when you've finished your ↗home-
work, | and had your ↗supper, | you're ↘tired, perhaps.
You're ⁻ready to go to ↘bed. You're ⁻ready for ↘bed.

For *certain, sure* and *likely* you may talk about football teams,
or other forms of sport.

⁻Are we (⁻Is our team) ↗certain (*or* ↗sure) to win
tomorrow? ↘No, | we're not ↘certain to win. We're ↘likely
to win.

You may ask about pupils who have been away through illness.

⁻Is David likely to come to ↗school tomorrow, | or is
he still too ↘ill?

[1] See § 33 above.

Pupils do not 'know' adjectives of this type by learning the meaning and nothing more. They must learn to use them in their patterns.

§ **132.** Many adjectives are closely linked with one or more prepositions. When, therefore, examples occur of an adjective used with a preposition, pupils should be helped to associate them. If the textbook provides only one example, provide others. Require your pupils to enter two or three examples in their notebooks. Complete sentences are more useful than a mere note of the adjective and the preposition, because different prepositions are appropriate in different contexts.

Afraid of and *ready for* have been given above. A good dictionary will supply examples. If you wish to be ready, at any time, to provide examples, you may make your own collection, indexed in alphabetical order. You will have specimens (in sentences) such as 'anxious *for* news', 'anxious *about* his health', 'aware *of* the facts', 'angry *with* someone *for* doing something'.

§ **133.** Many adjectives are used in a pattern with a clause, the conjunction *that* usually being omitted. This item is not easily drilled through questions and answers. You may, however, collect examples, as for prepositions, and use these as specimens when an adjective occurs in this pattern in reading-texts. You may also make incidental statements and ask questions with adjectives in this pattern. Here are suggestions:

I'm ‾glad (that) you're ⌄well again.

I'm ‾sorry you've been ⌄ill.

Are you ‾glad you're going to ⌁X?

‾Are(n't) you sorry you're ⌁not going to X?[1]

§ **134.** The use of participial adjectives to modify nouns is common. There is no special difficulty so far as meaning is concerned. Your pupils will quickly see that 'a terrifying experience' is one that terrifies the persons concerned, and 'terrified people' are people who are or have been terrified.

---

[1] This is a good opportunity for using the interrogative-negative type of question, expecting the answer 'Yes'. If this type of question causes difficulty, explain that 'Yes' must precede an answer in the affirmative (e.g. 'Yes, I am'), and give further examples from time to time.

The use of nouns and gerunds to modify nouns presents problems of stress, and your pupils will need help. If your pupils go hiking or mountaineering they may use sleeping-bags. If they use this compound, they must place a stress on the first element only: *a 'sleeping-bag*. This is an example of the gerund: a bag for sleeping in. Compare *a 'sleeping 'child*. This is the participial adjective: a child who is sleeping. There are stresses on both words. If you help your pupils to analyse such pairs of words for meaning, you will enable them to use stresses correctly. They will know that the compound *sewing-machine* has a primary stress on *sew*, that *walking-stick* has the stress on *walk*, and that in *smiling faces* there are equal stresses on the first syllable of *smiling* and the first syllable of *faces: 'smiling 'faces*. If a pupil says *'flying 'field*, ask whether this means 'a field for flying' or 'a field that flies'. He will then, you may hope, realize that he must say *'flying-field*. If he talks about a *'flying fox* (stress on the participle only), again ask him what a flying fox is. It is a fox that flies, and *flying* is an adjective. There must be a stress on each word: *a 'flying 'fox*.

There is no need to use the grammatical terms. Analysis of meaning is easier and more effective in achieving results. The native speaker of English makes the analysis unconsciously and places his stresses automatically.

§ **135.** This is not the place for a full treatment of stress and the related problems of pitch and intonation. For information on these questions other books may be consulted. A few words on the combination of noun and noun may be helpful, however.

In the pattern *noun × noun* meaning 'something made of something', there are equal stresses: *a 'gold 'watch; 'leather 'shoes: a 'cotton 'shirt*. There are equal stresses, too, when the two nouns indicate that one thing is to be identified with another: *a 'baby 'boy; 'women 'doctors* (women who are doctors); *a 'child 'actor*.

In the pattern *noun × noun* meaning 'something used or intended for something else', there is stress on the first element only: *a 'cotton-mill; 'shoe polish; a 'key-ring*.

The use or non-use of hyphens is not a safe guide to stress position. *A 'paper 'bag* is a bag made of paper; *a 'paper-knife* (not always printed with a hyphen) is a knife used for cutting paper. If one of your pupils were to say *a 'paper 'knife*, with equal stresses, it is unlikely that this would lead to misunderstanding, but wrong use of stress and pitch marks the speaker as 'a foreigner' much more than inaccurate vowel sounds.

There are many other stress problems in combinations of noun and noun. Compare '*slave-driver*, a man in charge of slaves, and '*woman* '*driver*, a woman who is a driver of cars (the same stress pattern as in '*baby* '*boy*, '*woman* '*teacher*). You, as a teacher, must be aware of these problems and should be prepared to give guidance when it is needed.

§ **136.** Compounds of the type *blue-eyed*, *long-haired* and *bare-footed* may occur in reading-texts at this stage. When examples do occur, you may call attention to two points.

(i) Meaning: *a blue-eyed girl* is a girl with blue eyes. The form *eyed* is from the noun *eye* and not from the (rare) verb *to eye*.

(ii) Stress pattern: double stress, as in a '*white-*'*haired man; a* '*four-engined* '*aircraft*.

Similar compounds are freely made by putting together an adverb and a participle: *a* '*well-*'*dressed* '*woman*, a woman who is dressed well; '*badly-behaved* '*children*, children who behave badly.

Give other examples, and call attention to the equal stresses.

IF-CLAUSES (2)
UNLESS; IN CASE (OF); WHETHER

§ **137.** *If*-clauses are dealt with in Chapter Eight. The examples are limited to clauses referring to future time and to unfulfilled or impossible conditions (present or future time). Now that pupils have learnt the Past Perfect Tense,[1] it is possible to present sentences dealing with unfulfilled conditions in past time, as 'If I had gone from here to X by air, it would have taken me only eight hours'.

§ **138.** The tenses used in this type of sentence require the use of the Past Perfect Tense in the *if*-clause and the Conditional Perfect Tense in the main clause. Several weak forms are usual even at ordinary speed. You may speak slowly and carefully when first presenting the new material, but after this material is familiar it is desirable to increase your speed of utterance until you are using the weak forms. Here are examples with phonemic transcriptions.

If I'd (= I had) known, I'd (= I would) have told you.
if aid ⟋noun, | aid əv ⟍tould ju:.

Note that in *I'd* (and *you'd, we'd, he'd, she'd, they'd*), the *'d* may represent either *had* or *would*, according as it occurs in the *if*-clause or in the main clause. When your pupils have heard numerous examples, you may write specimen sentences on the blackboard, with the full forms in parentheses as in the example above, for pupils to copy into their notebooks.

If they'd (= they had) asked him, he'd (= he would) have been glad to help.
if ðeid ⟋a:skt him, | hi:d əv bin ⟍glad tə help.

Note, in this example, how the four words 'he would have been' are uttered together /hi:ədvbin:/, with the weak form /bin/ for *been*.

[1] Chapter Ten of this book.

You may help your pupils to acquire fluency in such groups by repeating /hi:dəvbin/ (or /aidəvbin/, /ʃi:dəvbin/, /wi:dəvbin/) several times in rapid succession, and then requiring your pupils to do the same, first in chorus and then individually.

If you'd (= you had) come to me, I could have helped you.

if ju:d ˊkʌm tə mi:, | ai kəd əv ˋhelpt ju:.

In this example the words 'I could have' are uttered together rapidly, on a low level pitch.

If you'd (= you had) been here, you'd (= you would) have seen me.

if ju:d ˊbi(:)n hiə, | ju:d əv ˋsi:n mi:.

There is a rise in pitch on *been* here (continuing until the end of the clause), and either the weak form /bin/ or the strong form /bi:n/ may be used.

§ 139. To present this new material recall and practise some of the material in §§ 67–70. After using examples with the Past Tense in the *if*-clause, use them again, with suitable additions (as suggested below) with the Past Perfect Tense in the *if*-clause.

ˉLook at this ˋglass. ˉWhat would happen if I ˋdropped it?ˉIt would ˋbreak, | ˋwouldn't it?

ˉWhat would you be able to ˋdo, | if I ˉgave you this ˋknife? You'd be able to ˉcut this ˋwood.

ˉHow long would it take me to get to the ˋstation, | if I took a ˋtaxi (*or* went by ˋbus)? It would take me ˉtwenty ˋminutes, | ˋwouldn't it?

Repeat these, or other sequences, and require answers from the class. Then, when you are satisfied with results, continue:

Look at that ˋglass. ˉDid I ˊdrop it? (ˋNo, | you ˋdidn't.) If I had ˊdropped it, | it would have /əv/ ˋbroken.

Repeat this sequence three or four times, and note the advice given in § 138 about slow and careful utterance, followed by utterance at normal speed with weak forms. Continue with other examples:

‾Did I go to (ꜛX)[1] yesterday? (ꜜNo, | you ꜜdidn't.) ‾If I had gone to (ꜛX) yesterday, | by ꜛtrain, | it would have taken me (‾two ꜜhours). If I had gone there by ꜛbus (*or* ꜛcar), it would have taken me (ꜜthree hours).

Repeat this sequence several times. You may now repeat the sequence with *you:* 'Did you go to (X) yesterday?' *etc.* If answers are not fluent and correct, give more examples.

‾If I asked you to lift this ꜛchair, | ‾could you ꜛlift it, Tom? (ꜜYes, | I ꜜcould.) ꜛDid I ask Tom to lift the chair, Paul?[2] (ꜜNo, | you ꜜdidn't.) ‾If I had asked Tom to lift the ꜛchair, | he could have ꜜlifted it. If I had asked ꜛPaul to lift it, | ꜜPaul could have lifted it. If I had asked ꜛJohn to lift it, | ꜜJohn could have lifted it.

‾If I asked you to lift this ꜜbook-case, David, | ‾could you ꜛlift it? (ꜜNo, | I ꜜcouldn't.) ꜛDid I ask you to lift it?[2] (ꜜNo, | you ꜜdidn't.) If I ꜛhad[3] asked David to lift it, | ‾could he have ꜛlifted it? ꜜNo, | he ꜜcouldn't. He ꜜcouldn't have lifted it. The book-case is ‾too ꜜheavy for David to lift.

Repeat the sequences but this time require answers to the final questions as well as to the preliminary questions.

‾If I had asked you to lift the ꜛbook-case, | ‾could you have ꜛlifted it? (ꜜNo, | I ꜜcouldn't.) ꜜLong answer, please. (ꜜNo, | I ꜜcouldn't have lifted it.)

[1] Supply a place, and times, to suit local conditions.

[2] Note that in this question there is continuous rise in pitch.

[3] Use the strong form /had/ here, because of the steep rise in pitch on *had*, used for emphasis.

§ **140.** Much more practice will probably be needed before your pupils use this kind of conditional sentence confidently. Five-minute drills well spaced out will be better than a drill occupying half an hour or longer. Vary the subject matter of the sequences to add interest and prevent the drills from becoming dull. You may, perhaps, ask questions about places and people likely to be known to your pupils.

⁻If you had gone to (⌐Agra) last month, | ⁻what places might you have ⌐visited there? (I might have visited (the Taj Ma⌐hal).)

⁻If you had gone to (⌐Tokyo) last year, | ⁻who(m) might you have ⌐seen? (I might have seen (the ⌐Emperor).)

§ **141.** The use of *unless* may be presented with the material in Chapter Eight, or, if *unless* does not occur in reading material at this stage, postponed. It is not difficult to find suitable contexts. The chief point for pupils to realize is that *if* is far more frequent than *unless*.[1] Thus, the statement 'You'll be late if you don't hurry' is more likely to be used than 'You'll be late unless you hurry', though this is, of course, quite possible and usual. *Unless* is more usual when the clause includes a passive construction from which the subject and the finite of *be* is dropped, as in: 'Unless required to do so, he preferred not to be present', or 'Unless compelled to stay indoors by the weather, they generally go for a walk every day'.

You will not talk to your class about this now, though when examples of this type occur in reading material you may perhaps call attention to them and give a brief comment.

§ **142.** Confine your presentation of *unless* to a few simple examples. Oral drills are not essential. If your pupils have a recognition knowledge of the word and its use, this is probably enough. When they themselves need conditional sentences, the use of *if . . . not* will be adequate.

[1] *The General Service List of English Words* (ed. Dr Michael West) gives an estimate of 8,046 occurrences of *if* and only 516 of *unless* in 5,000,000 words.

Talk about your own activities, or those of some other person (real or fictional).

I ⁻like ⮮swimming (playing ⮮tennis, ⮮walking, *etc.*). I ⁻usually go for a swim (play tennis, *etc.*) on ⮮Sundays, | if it doesn't ⮮rain. Un⁻less it ⮮rains, | I ⁻usually go for a swim on ⮮Sundays.

If this sequence is unsuitable, you may prefer this:

⁻What's to⮮day? (It's ⮮Tuesday.) ⁻What's to⮮morrow? (It's ⮮Wednesday.) ⁻Shall I be here to⮮morrow? ⮮Yes, | I ⮮shall. I shall be ⁻here tomorrow unless I'm ⮮ill. Unless I'm ⮮ill, | I shall be ⁻here to⮮morrow.

Note that of the two last statements the first is uttered without a pause, one intonation group, and that the second is uttered with a pause after *ill*, two intonation groups. You may use *I'll be* instead of *I shall be*. If you use *I shall be*, use the weak form of *shall:* /aiʃlbiː/.

Use *unless* for occasional statements in class.

⮮Now, Tom, | unless you ⮮work harder, | you'll ⁻fail in the exami⮮nation.

Unless you have any ⮮questions to ask, | we'll go on to (the ⮮next paragraph, the ⮮next section, *etc.*).

§ **143.** The phrase *in case* need not be presented until it occurs in reading-texts. When it does occur, oral presentation and examples are useful. It must be distinguished from the use of *if*.

In case introduces a possibility against which a precaution is advisable. For example: 'Take an umbrella with you in case it rains'. This suggests that it is advisable to have an umbrella because rain is possible. 'Take an umbrella with you if it rains' suggests that an umbrella should be taken if there is rain, but not if there is no rain.

This difference is better explained through examples which are translated. Here are specimens you may use:

ˉTake some ⟍money with you, | in ˉcase you see some-thing you'd like to ⟍buy.

When you're reading an ⟋English book, | it's useful to have a ⟍dictionary, | in ˉcase you find words you don't ⟍know.

With *in case* you may present the phrase *in case of*. Two or three examples will be enough. Perhaps there is a fire-alarm in the school building (or elsewhere). On such fire-alarms in England, there might be this notice:

In case of fire, break the glass and pull the handle (to give the alarm).

'In case of fire' means 'in the event of fire', 'if fire should break out'. This may be explained in the mother tongue.

Another example might be this notice:

In case of rain (*or* bad weather), the sports meeting will be postponed.

These examples of *in case of* will help your pupils to form the right associations with *in case*, and to see the difference between *in case* and *if*.

§ **144.** The conjunction *whether* may, in some contexts, be replaced by *if*. When you first present *whether* it is probably advisable not to give examples in which *if* may be used as an alternative. When examples with *if* occur in reading material, tell your class about this use, and pass on the information given below in §§ 148–9.

Whether introduces indirect questions that begin with one of the twenty-four anomalous finites.[1] Your pupils are familiar with indirect questions introduce by *how many*, *when* and *which*,[2] and by *what*.[3]

Before presenting *whether* recall some of this material (using *ask* and *tell* with *what*, *where*, and *how many*).

[1] Listed in the table on p. 2 of *A Guide to Patterns and Usage*.

[2] See § 93, *Stage Two*.

[3] See §§ 131–134, *Stage Two*.

ˉHow many ↘doors are there in this room, Paul? (There are ↘two.) ˉWhat did I ↘ask Paul? I asked him ˉhow many ↘doors there are in this room.

ˉWhat have I in my ↘hand, John? (You have a ↘book.) ˉWhat did I ↘ask John? I asked him ˉwhat I have in my ↘hand.

ˉWhere's ↘your book, David? (It's on my ↘desk.) ˉWhat did I ↘ask David? I asked him ˉwhere his ↘book is.

My pen is in my ↘pocket. ˉWhat have I just ↘told you? I've told you ˉwhere my ↘pen is. It's in my ↘pocket.

Continue in this way until you are confident that your pupils are familiar with this type of question and statement. Use the material given in *Stage Two*, with any additional vocabulary items that have been acquired since.

§ **145.** Now introduce *whether*. Ask questions that begin with one of the anomalous finites.

I have a ↘pen in my pocket. ˉHave I a ↗pencil in my pocket, | ↗too? You don't ↘know. You don't ↘know whether I have a pencil in my pocket.

Repeat the last question several times. Then produce a pencil.

↘Yes, | I have a ↘pencil in my pocket. Here it ↘is.

Continue with other questions, and require pupils to ask questions.

ˉHave I any ↗keys in my pocket. You don't ↘know whether I have any keys in my pocket. ↘John, | ˉask me whether I have any ↘keys in my pocket. (ˉHave you any ↗keys in your pocket?) ↘Yes, | I ↘have. ˉHere they ↘are. ˉWhat did John ↘ask me, Paul? (He asked you ˉwhether you have any ↘keys in your pocket.)

ˉWill[1] you come to school on ⌐Monday, Jane? (ˣYes, | I
ˣwill.[1]) ˉWhat did I ˣask Jane? I asked her ˉwhether she
will come to school on ˣMonday. ˉWhat did I ˣask you,
Jane? (You asked me ˉwhether I will[1] come to school on
ˣMonday.)

Many further sequences will probably be necessary before pupils
use this new item confidently and correctly. If pupils answer
hesitatingly and make errors, ask and answer questions yourself,
but as soon as pupils gain confidence, give them opportunities of
using complete sequences themselves while you listen. Tell pupils to
make statements and put questions to their classmates.

§ **146.** Presentation of this new item may be spread over several
weeks, ten to fifteen minutes at a time. During the later drills introduce
can, do, must, have to and other items that are already known.

ˉCan you speak (Chi⌐nese), Susan? (ˣNo, | I ˣcan't.)
ˉWhat did I ˣask Susan? I asked her ˉwhether she can
speak (Chiˣnese).

ˉDo you go to the cinema every ⌐evening, Joan? (ˣNo, | I
ˣdon't.) ˉWhat did I ˣask you, Joan? (You asked me
ˉwhether I go to the cinema every ˣevening.) ˣLucy, | ˉwhat
did I ˣask Joan? (You asked her ˉwhether she goes to the
ˣcinema every evening.)

ˉDoes school begin at ⌐six o'clock, Lucy? (ˣNo, | it
ˣdoesn't.) ˉWhat did I ˣask you, Lucy? (You asked me
ˉwhether school begins at ˣsix o'clock.) ˣHelen, | ˉdid
Lucy answer ⌐'Yes' | or ˣ'No'? (She answered ˣ'No'.)
ˉWhat time ˣdoes school begin, Helen?[2] (It begins at ˣnine
o'clock.)

[1] Or *shall*.

[2] Because there is a fall in pitch on *does* the strong form /dʌz/ is needed
here.

§ 147. At a later stage give examples of *whether . . .* followed by *or whether*.

ˉDo you come to school by ∕bus, Tom, | or do you ∖walk? (I ∖walk.) ˉWhat did I ∖ask Tom? I asked him ˉwhether he comes to school by ∕bus, | or whether he ∖walks.

Note that *whether* is repeated when there are two direct questions, each with its finite verb, linked by *or*. Compare the following, in which there is an alternative question with *or*, but only one finite verb.

ˉDo you come to school at ∕eight o'clock | or at ∖nine o'clock, Tom? (I come to school at ∖nine o'clock.) ˉWhat did I ∖ask Tom? I asked him whether he comes to school at ∕eight o'clock | or at ∖nine o'clock.

This repetition of *whether* in cases where each of two direct questions linked by *or* includes a finite verb may need explanation.

§ 148. When pupils have learnt this use of *whether* you may give examples in which *if* is used in place of *whether*. This is a common colloquial use and pupils should be familiar with it. You may ask questions such as these:

Bruce isn't ∖here this morning. Does ˉanyone know if he's ∕ill? Have ˉyou ever been up in an ∕aeroplane, David? (∖No, | I ∖haven't.) ˉWhat did I ∖ask David? I asked him if he has ˉever been up in an ∖aeroplane.

ˉHave you read 'Robinson ∕Crusoe', Roger?[1] (∖Yes, | I ∖have.) ˉWhat did I ∖ask Roger? I asked him ˉif he has read 'Robinson ∖Crusoe'.

ˉDid you play ∕football yesterday, Tom? (∖Yes, | I ∖did.) ˉWhat did I ∖ask you, Tom? (You asked me if I played ∖football yesterday.)

[1] Use a title likely to be known.

§ **149.** In some situations the use of *if* for *whether* is undesirable. It may lead to misunderstanding. Such situations are not likely in classroom work, but if, in reading-texts, such a situation occurs, you may need to give an explanation. Compare:

(i) Please write and let me know if you are coming.

(ii) Please write and let me know whether you are coming.

In (i), which is conditional, there is a request for an answer *only* if the answer is 'Yes, I am coming'. If the answer is 'No', an answer is not necessary.

In (ii), which is alternative, there is a definite request for an answer, either 'Yes, I am coming' or 'No, I am not coming'.

CHAPTER SIXTEEN (§§ 150–156)

SOME PATTERNS FOR *WISH*
BE SORRY (*THAT*); *BE A PITY* (*THAT*)

§ **150.** Your pupils are now familiar with conditional clauses in which there are unfulfilled conditions. They have heard sentences such as 'If I had ten thousand pounds, I could travel round the world, buy a new house, *etc.*', 'If you went to Washington, you might see the President'.[1]

This use of the Past Tense (*had* and *went* in the examples above) for present or future time is not restricted to conditional clauses. It occurs after the verb *wish*. This verb is used in several patterns, and these need to be presented carefully. Unless this is done pupils may use *wish* in contexts where it is quite inappropriate. If a person enters a shop in London and says 'I wish a fountain-pen' he is at once recognized as a foreigner. Even the request 'I wish to see some fountain-pens' is less usual than 'I'd like to see (*or* Please show me) some fountain-pens'. The pattern in which *wish* is most frequently used is that in which the verb is followed by a clause (with *that* omitted) having a verb in a Past Tense, as 'I wish I *were* rich', 'I wish I *had* ten thousand pounds', 'She wishes she *could* speak Spanish'.

§ **151.** To present this use of *wish* you may start from material already familiar, the *if*-clause. Or you may use *be sorry* (*that*) or *It's a pity* (*that*). Here are procedures that start with *if*-clauses. They have the advantage of revising and practising previously learnt material. Translation of the first few sequences may be helpful and economical of time.

I ⁻haven't (got) a \motor-car.[2] If I had a /motor-car, | I ⁻wouldn't have to come to school by \bus (\tram).[3] I ⁻wish

[1] See § 69 above.

[2] Substitute *My friend X* if you prefer, and make the necessary changes (of pronouns, *etc.*) throughout, and say *go to his \office, etc.*

[3] Or \walk to school.

I had a ˇcar. But I ˇhaven't (got) a car. I have to come to
school by ˇbus (ˇtram).

I've ‾never been to ˇParis.[1] If I had a lot of ˊmoney, | I
could ‾go to ˇParis. I ‾wish I could go to ˇParis. I ‾wish I
had enough money to go to ˇParis. But I ˇhaven't enough
money to go to Paris.

Have ˊyou enough money to go to Paris, George?
(ˇNo, | I ˇhaven't.) ‾Do you wish you ˊhad enough money
to go to Paris? (ˇYes, | I ˇdo.)

I'd ˇlike to go to Paris.[2] I'd ‾like to read French ˇbooks.
But I ‾don't ˇknow French. If I ˊknew French, | I could
‾read French ˇbooks. I ‾wish I knew ˇFrench. But I ˇdon't
know French. I ‾can't ˇread French.

Do ˊyou know French, Tom? (ˇNo, | I ˇdon't.) ‾Do
you (or ‾Don't you) wish you ˊknew French? (ˇYes, | I
ˇdo.)

You probably know which pupils in your class are not quite good
enough to be members of the football team, or other teams.

‾Are you a member of the ˊfootball team, Harry?
(ˇNo, | I'm ˇnot.) ‾Do you wish you ˊwere a member of
the team? (ˇYes, | I ˇdo.) You'd ˇlike to be a member of
the team, | ˇwouldn't you?

If you are unfortunate enough not to have any wall pictures or
maps (or a clock) in your classroom, this will provide a useful
sequence. Perhaps your pupils cannot afford good reference books.

‾Have we a map of ˊEngland on the walls of our class-
room, Mary? (ˇNo, | we ˇhaven't.) I wish we ˇhad a map
of England. It would be ˇuseful, | ˇwouldn't it?

[1] Or any other place you may prefer.
[2] This use of *like* is dealt with in § 69 above.

ˉHave you a good English ⌃dictionary, Susan? (˅No, | I ˅haven't.) ˉDon't you wish you ⌃had a good dictionary, Susan? (˅Yes, | I ˅do.)

§ **152.** Here are procedures for presenting *wish* with *be sorry*, *be a pity*.

ˉHave you a good English ⌃dictionary, Edith? (˅No, | I ˅haven't.) I'm ˅sorry you haven't a dictionary. A dictionary is very ˅useful. I ˉwish you had a ˅dictionary.

ˉHave we a map of ⌃England on the walls of our classroom, John? (˅No, | we ˅haven't.) It's a ˅pity we haven't a map of England. A map would be ˅useful. I ˉwish we ˅had one. (*etc., etc.*)

§ **153.** Present sequences with the Past Perfect Tense after *wish*, corresponding to *if*-clauses with unfulfilled conditions in the past.[1]
Classroom situations for this are not easy to find. You may find it possible to use local happenings.

There was a good ˅film at the Ritz cinema last week. I didn't ˅know about it. If I ⌃had known about it, | I should have gone to ˅see it.[2] I ˉwish I had ˅known about it.

My brother ˉlikes to see ˅boxing matches. There was a ˉgood boxing match last ˅month. But my brother ˉdidn't ˅know about it. If he ⌃had known about it, | he'd have /hi:d əv/ ˉgone to ˅see it. He ˉwishes he ˅had known about it.

You will find occasional opportunities for using this item when pupils make errors.

[1] See Chapter Fifteen of this book.

[2] See § 138 for the weak forms used at normal speed. Here the strong form /had/ is used for emphasis.

You've made some ⁻bad misˋtakes. ⁻Why didn't you ask me to ˎhelp you? If you'd ʃasked me, | I'd have ˎhelped you, | ˎgladly. I wish you ˎhad asked me.

§ 154. Be careful not to use *I wish* in classroom situations where it is inappropriate. When you need to maintain order the imperative is more suitable. 'Be quiet!' and 'No talking, please!' are suitable. 'I wish you'd be quiet' and 'I wish you'd stop talking' are unsuitable. This is because the words *I wish* are often used to introduce what is unlikely to be realized, as in 'I wish I were rich' or 'She wishes she were beautiful'. If, therefore, you say 'I wish you'd be quiet', it suggests that you have little expectation of being obeyed. A weak-willed mother may say to her unruly children, 'I *do* wish you'd stop making so much noise'. A mother who expects and obtains obedience says, 'Be quiet!', 'Stop making so much noise'.

§ 155. Other patterns in which *wish* is used are less important. *Wish* is used with an infinitive, as in 'The headmaster wishes to see you'. *Would like* is preferable in contexts where the object of the wish is not certainly to be achieved, as in 'He would like to go to Europe'. *Wish* is used in the pattern: *wish somebody something*. Give a few examples:

I wish you a pleasant journey.

He wished me success in my plans.

Do not teach *wish for* until examples occur in reading materials. You do not want your pupils to say 'I wish for your help' or 'I wish for a bicycle'. *Wish for* is used chiefly in contexts where the wish is something that comes by good fortune, not as the result of will-power or effort. Make this clear to your pupils when examples occur.

The weather during the holidays was ⁻everything we could ˎwish for.

Mrs X is a ⁻very lucky ˎwoman. She has ⁻everything that a woman can ˎwish for: | a handsome ʃhusband, | clever ʃchildren, | a fine ʃhouse, | and ⁻lots of ˎmoney.

§ **156.** The choice of 'the right word' is often difficult unless vocabulary items are learnt and used in suitable contexts and situations. The verb *want* is, according to *A General Service List of English Words*, twice as frequent as the verb *wish*. *Do you want (me) to* and *Would you like (me) to* are certainly more frequent than *Do you wish (me) to*. *Wish for* is of low frequency and restricted in its use.

The material in this chapter is not easily presented in drills. You should, instead, give examples of normal usage and make comments on these in the language of your pupils. Give further comments when examples occur in reading material.

SO × ADJECTIVE × *THAT*
SUCH . . . THAT; SUCH . . . AS

§ 157. *So* has been presented as an adverb of degree in the pattern *not so* × *adj.* × *as*.[1] *So* is also used in the patterns *so* × *adj.* × *that*, and *so much* (*many*) *that*. Procedures for presenting these patterns follow.

§ 158. Start by using a pattern that is already known, the patterns *too* × adj. × *to*-infinitive, and adj. × *enough* × *to*-infinitive.[2]

This bookcase is ˅heavy, | ˅very heavy. It's ⁻too heavy for me to ˅lift. It's ⁻so heavy that I can't ˅lift it.

⁻Can you touch the ⁄ceiling, Tom? (˅No, | I ˅can't.) ⁻Why can't Tom touch the ˅ceiling, David? (It's ⁻too ˅high for him to touch.) ˅Yes, | that's ˅right. The ceiling's ⁻so high that Tom can't ˅touch it.

Produce a thin stick, easily broken, and a thick piece of wood that cannot be broken. Recall and practice the use of *could* in *if*-clauses.

⁻Look at this ˅stick. Is it ⁄thick | or ˅thin, Peter? (It's ˅thin.) ⁻Could you ⁄break it?[3] ⁻Could you ⁄break it, | if you ⁄tried? (˅Yes, | I ˅could.) ˅Break it, then. ⁻What has Peter just ˅done, David? (He's ⁻broken the ˅stick.)

⁻Look at this piece of ˅wood. ⁻Is this piece of wood ⁄thin | or ˅thick, John? (It's ˅thick.) ˅Yes, | this piece of wood is ˅thick. It's ⁻too thick for you to ˅break. It's ⁻not

[1] See *Stage Two*, Chapter Twenty-eight.

[2] See *Stage Two*, Chapter Twelve.

[3] See § 68 in this book.

ˎthin enough for you to break. ˎI'm going to try to break it. I ˎcan't. It's ¯so thick that I can't ˎbreak it.

Note that in all these examples the conjunction *that* should be uttered with the weak form /ðət/.

its ¯sou θik ðət ai kaːnt ˎbreik it.

§ 159. You will be able to provide other sequences from local conditions and happenings. Some of the following may be possible.

¯Are the buses (trams) in this town sometimes ˊcrowded? (ˎYes, | they ˎare.) At ¯what time are they ˎmost crowded? They're most crowded between ¯five and six o'ˎclock, | when people are going ˎhome, | from ˎwork.[1] They're sometimes ¯so crowded that there are no ˎseats. We sometimes have to ˎstand.

Mary's not at ˎschool today. She's ˎill. She's ¯so ill that she has to stay in ˎbed. She's ¯so ill that she can't come to ˎschool.

Perhaps you can exhibit some fruit, either very unripe or too bad to eat, or a worn-out article of clothing.

¯Look at these ˎmangoes (ˎapples). Are they ˊripe? (ˎNo, | they're ˎnot.) They're ¯not ripe enough to ˎeat. They're ¯so green (sour, hard) that they're not good to ˎeat.

¯Look at this ˎcoat. It's very ˎold, | ˎisn't it? It's full of ˎholes. It's ˎdirty. It's ¯so old that no one will ˎwear it.

When your pupils have heard numerous sequences of this kind, require pupils in turn to produce them. Give them the stick, the piece of wood, *etc.*, and tell them to reproduce your statements, and ask questions to be answered by their classmates. (This procedure is

[1] Give the times of the local rush hours.

necessary here. You cannot ask questions that require, in the answers, the pattern you are presenting. If you ask the question, 'How thick is this stick?', you cannot expect the answer 'It's so thick that I can't break it'.)

§ **160.** Next present examples with *many*.

ˉWhen do we see the ⵠstars? ˉDo we see them during the ⵠday, | or only during the ⵠnight? (We see them only during the ⵠnight.) ˉCan we ⵠcount the stars, Betty? (ⵠNo, | we ⵠcan't.) It's imⵠpossible to count the stars.[1] There are ˉso many stars that we can't ⵠcount them.

Give other sequences by talking about the leaves of trees (perhaps there are trees to be seen from the classroom window), the books in the school library (if you are fortunate enough to have more than your pupils will want to count), the number of words in the English language, or whatever else your imagination enables you to supply.

ˉHow many English ⵠwords do you know? You know about ˉone ⵠthousand, perhaps. ˉHow many words are there in this English ⵠdictionary? There are ⵠtwenty thousand.[2] ˉHow many words are there in the English ⵠlanguage? I don't ⵠknow. There are ˉso many words that we can't ⵠcount them.

§ **161.** Give some examples with *few* and plural nouns (in contrast with *little*).[3] Bring to class a twig or small branch on which the leaves can easily be counted.

ˉHow many leaves are there on a big ⵠtree? There are

---

[1] The purpose of these preliminary statements is to revise recently presented items, here the pattern dealt with is § 33 in this book.

[2] There is no need to be precise. Use any suitably large figure.

[3] See *Stage Two*, Chapter Twenty-seven. It is useful to recall and practise the difference between *few* and *little*.

ˉso many that we can't ˅count them. ˉLook at this small ˅branch. There are very ˅few leaves on it. There are ˉso few that I can ˅count them. There are only ˅ten leaves on this branch.

Hold up a book.

ˉHow many ˅words are there in this book? There are ˉso many words that I can't ˅count them.

Now open the book and point to the title-page.

ˉAre there a lot of words on this ⁄page? ˅No, | there are ˉso few words that I can ˅count them. There are only ˅twenty words on this page.

§ 162. *Much* is used with 'uncountable' nouns. *Money* provides useful examples.

Motor-cars cost a ˉlot of ˅money, | ˅don't they? They cost ˉso much money that most people can't ˅buy them.

Travel by ˅air costs a lot of money, | ˅too. It costs ˉso much that most people have to travel by ˅train, | or by ˅steamer.

Food and other products may provide further examples. Make your examples refer to your own country, or neighbouring countries.

ˉWhat's the chief crop in ˅Thailand? It's ˅rice, | ˅isn't it? Thailand grows ˉso much rice that it's able to sell rice to ˅other countries.

ˉWhich country is famous for ˅wool? Do you ⁄know? (Aus˅tralia is.) ˅Yes, | Australia produces ˉso much wool that it ˅sells most of it, | to countries in ˅Europe, | and ˅Asia.

As with all teaching items, it is important to give occasional examples after the first presentation. Pupils are unlikely to learn them well unless there is repetition. If, therefore, you see an opportunity for using this particular item during the months that follow, do so. If there is heavy rain followed by floods, you may say:

We've had a lot of ˅rain this week, | ˅haven't we? (*Or* They had a lot of ˅rain in X last week, | ˅didn't they?) There's been[1] ˉso much rain that the town is ˅flooded. (*Or* There was ˉso much rain that there were ˅floods.)

If there is a drought, you may give an example with *little*.

It's a ˉvery long time since we had ˅rain, | ˅isn't it? We've had ˉso little rain that the ˅crops are poor.

A good teacher is always on the alert for opportunities of this sort. These opportunities, if seen and taken, not only keep teaching items fresh in the minds of his pupils, but also prove to pupils that their knowledge of English is becoming adequate for dealing with everyday topics.

§ 163. *Such* is used in a pattern similar to one of the patterns for *so*. We may say 'It was so hot that I couldn't sleep'. We may say, 'It was such a hot night that I couldn't sleep'. When, therefore, you present *such*, you may use *so* as a starting-point.

ˉLook at this ˅book. It's ˅large, | ˅isn't it? It's ˉtoo large to go in my ˅pocket. It's ˉso large that I can't put it in my ˅pocket.

This is ˉsuch a large book that I can't put it in my ˅pocket.

After repeating the last sentence two or three times you may write on the blackboard the two main sentences, that with *so large that* and that with *such a large book that*. You may call attention to the fact that *such* precedes the indefinite article. If you are giving grammatical information, you may point out that *so* is an adverb of

---

[1] = *There has been* /ðəzbin/.

degree, that *such* is an adjective, and that the clauses are clauses of result. This kind of information is necessary, however, only if your Syllabus, or examinations taken by your pupils, include grammar.

Give further examples, including plural nouns.

‾Look at ⌄these books. They're ⌄small, | and ⌄thin, | ⌄aren't they? They're ‾so small that I can put ⌄three of them in my pocket.

These are ‾such small books that I can put ⌄three of them in my pocket.

‾Who's the best ⌄runner in this class? (⌄Paul is.) ⌄Yes, | Paul's ‾such a good runner that no one can ⌄catch him (*or* that he always wins ⌄races).

Write on the blackboard:

Paul runs so fast that no one can catch him.
Paul is such a good runner that no one can catch him.

§ 164. *Such* is also used followed by *as*. Again you may use *so* as a starting-point.[1] Call upon two pupils to hold up books (or other articles) different in size.

‾Look at ⌄Paul's book. It's ⌄large, | ⌄isn't it? ⌄David has a book, ⌄too. David's book ‾isn't so (*or* as) large as ⌄Paul's book. It ‾isn't such a large book as ⌄Paul's.

Again write the last two sentences on the blackboard, to be copied into notebooks, so that pupils have a record of the two patterns.

Perhaps you can show green or unripe fruit. Give the complete statement, followed by one in which *as* and what follows is omitted.

‾Look at these ⌄apples. They're ⌄hard, | and ⌄green. They're not ⌄ripe. They're not good to ⌄eat. I don't ⌄like

[1] Use *not so . . . as* or *not as . . . as*. Use *such . . . as* only in negative sentences.

such green apples as these. I don't ⌄like such green apples.
Do ⌁you like such green apples, Tom?

§ **165.** *Such as* is often used before words that name specimens
of a class. When this use first occurs in reading material, give other
examples. Here are specimens:

Countries in the north of Europe, such as Norway,
Sweden, Finland, Denmark . . .

Languages which come from Latin, such as Italian,
French, Spanish, and Portuguese . . .

Hard woods, such as teak and mahogany . . .

This use, and others not dealt with in this chapter, are best dealt
with as the need arises. Use *such* incidentally when opportunities
occur, for example, by saying:

⎺Don't be in such a ⌄hurry!
⎺Don't make such careless mis⌄takes!

In many cases the situation will make the meaning clear.

RELATIVE CLAUSES

§ **166.** The presentation of relative clauses needs to be spread over a long period of time. There is a wide variety of such clauses and some kinds are of much higher frequency and much greater importance than others. Some kinds may be presented orally and practised in oral drills. Other kinds seldom occur in speech (unless when read aloud from a script), and can be dealt with only from the printed page and in written exercises.

§ **167.** It is essential for the teacher to have a clear understanding of these differences. A fairly full treatment is given in *A Guide to Patterns and Usage*, § 94 (pp. 163–173). Teachers who wish to study the subject further may read Chapter XXXIV of Jespersen's *Essentials of English Grammar*.

A few grammatical terms are useful. Whether these are to be given to pupils or not is a question for teachers to decide. The syllabus, or the contents of public examinations, may make it necessary to do so. In general pupils should not be troubled by more than a minimum of terminology.

§ **168.** There are two main classes of relative clauses, defining and non-defining (or, in Jespersen's terminology, restrictive and non-restrictive). A defining clause is essential to the meaning of the sentence. In the sentence 'This is the boy who broke the window', the clause defines and makes precise *the boy*, which is the antecedent of the clause *who broke the window*. A non-defining clause is not essential. It may be omitted and the sentence will still make sense. A non-defining clause supplies additional but not essential information. In the sentence, 'This boy, who lives in Station Road, broke a window in the school', the clause *who lives in Station Road* may be omitted. A non-defining clause is marked off by a comma or commas (or placed in parentheses or after a dash or between dashes). Defining clauses are not marked off in these ways.

§ **169.** The relative pronoun may be omitted from a clause if it is the object of the verb or of a preposition. In *the boy I met yesterday* the pronoun *whom* is omitted; in *the book I bought yesterday* the pronoun *that* (or *which*) is omitted; in *the boy I was talking to* the pronoun *whom* is omitted. The clause is, by this omission, closer to its antecedent. Such clauses are known as contact-clauses. They are very frequent in both speech and writing. It is important for pupils to become familiar with them and to use them confidently. It would be wrong for teachers to tell their pupils that such clauses, with the relatives omitted, are typical only of colloquial use or 'incorrect'.

§ **170.** If you have used all the material in *Stage Two* your pupils will have heard and used simple examples of contact clauses. They are presented in §§ 4–7 of *Stage Two* and the relative pronoun omitted is *that* or *which*. Recall this material now.

ˉLook at these three ↘books. I'm going to put them ↘down. I've put one of them on ↗my desk. I've put one on ↘Paul's desk. I've put one on ↘Peter's desk.

The book I put on ↗my desk | is ↘green. The book I put on ↗Paul's desk | is ↘brown. The book I put on ↗Peter's desk | is ↘yellow.

ˉWhat colour is the book I put on ↗my desk? ↘Long answer, please, John. (The book you put on ↗your desk | is ↘green.) (*etc., etc.*)

§ **171.** In the sequences given in the section above the omitted relative is *that* or *which*. It is the object of the verb in the clause: *the book* (*that*) *I put on my desk.* The presentation of a large number of examples, and repeated drills, will be necessary. You may, if you wish, tell the class about the structure of the sentence. You may write on the blackboard:

I put a book on my desk.

The book (that) I put on my desk is green.

You may say that as the verb *put* has, in the second sentence, the relative *that* as its object, it is wrong to place *it* after *put*. This is an error commonly made by pupils. But if your pupils, after hearing and using the new pattern, do not make this error, do not give the warning. It is always unwise to discuss errors that are not made and often unwise to discuss errors that are made. Drills of what is correct are preferable to analysis of error.

You may say the choice between the two pronouns *that* and *which* is not important. *That* is perhaps preferable, as more frequently used, but there are no reliable statistics.

Give more sequences, using a variety of sentence patterns. Use examples in which the antecedents are nouns standing for things, not persons, and postpone for the present prepositional usages (as in 'the picture I am looking *at*').

§ 172. Suggestions follow:

ˇAlan, | ˉshow me a ˇbook. ˉWhat ˇcolour is the book Alan showed me? The book Alan showed me is ˇred.[1]

ˇJohn, | ˉplease hold up a ˇpencil. ˉWhat ˇcolour is the pencil John held up? The pencil he held up is ˇyellow.

ˇBruce, | ˉgive Paul a ˇpencil. ˉWhat colour is the pencil Bruce gave ˇPaul? The pencil Bruce gave Paul is ˇgreen.

ˇArthur, | ˉgive a pencil to the boy sitting beˇhind you. ˉWhat colour is the pencil Arthur gave to the boy sitting beˇhind him? The pencil Arthur gave to the boy sitting behind him is ˇblue.

Note that in these sequences you have used three sentence patterns:
1. V × I.O. × D.O.
2. V × D.O. × Adverb.
3. V × D.O. × *to* × I.O.
It is important to recall and revise previously learnt patterns when teaching new items. Unless there is regular recall and practice of this sort pupils may not retain what they have learnt.

§ 173. Repeat these sequences with variations (different objects, other verbs), making statements, asking and answering questions

---

[1] You use the long and complete answer so that the relative clause is repeated from the question. The short answer (It's red) would not help your pupils.

yourself. Then repeat the sequences and require answers from pupils.

˅Mary, | ˉshow me a ˅book. ˉWhat ˅colour is the book you showed me?[1] ˅Long answer, please. (The book I showed you is ˅blue.)

When pupils answer confidently and correctly, require pupils to make requests and ask questions to be answered by their class-mates. This last stage, in which the pupils do all the speaking while you listen, is the most useful.

§ **174.** The next step is the presentation of relative clauses in which the pronoun is the subject of the clause. Start with examples in which the antecedents are nouns standing for things, not persons. Use *that* as the relative, and tell the class, after the presentation, that *which* may also be used. Use the weak form of *that* /ðət/; the strong form /ðæt/ is seldom used.

Avoid using finites of *be* in the clauses when these are unnecessary. There is nothing wrong grammatically with 'the book that is on the table', 'the pencil that is on my desk'. But it is much more usual to say 'the book on the table' and 'the pencil on my desk'.[2] Avoid using finites of *have* in your clauses if it would be more idiomatic to use *with*. It is more usual to say 'the table with a broken leg' than 'the table that has a broken leg'.[3] You have taught your pupils to use these phrases. Do not now teach them to use patterns that are infrequently used. Here are suitable sequences. Hold up two envelopes in which letters have been delivered to you.

Here are ˉtwo ˅letters. One of them came to me ˅yester-day. The other came to me this ˅morning.

The letter that came ˄yesterday | is from my ˅brother. The letter that came this ˄morning | is from a friend in (˅Delhi).

---

[1] Or *are showing me* if Mary continues to hold up her book.

[2] See *Stage Two*, §§ 1–2, and Table No. 1.

[3] See *Stage Two*, § 3, and Table No. 3.

Hold up two pieces of chalk, one long (and therefore likely to break when dropped), the other very short (and unlikely to break when dropped).

¯Look at these two pieces of ⌄chalk. I'm going to ⌄drop them, | on my ⌄desk. I've ⌄dropped them. ¯Have they ⌄both broken? ⌄No. Only ⌄one of them has broken. The piece of chalk that ⌄broke | was the ⌄long piece. The piece that ⌄didn't break | was the ⌄short piece.

Hold up two more pieces of chalk, both long.

Here are two ⌄more pieces of chalk. I'm going to drop this piece to the ⌄floor. I've ⌄dropped it. It has ⌄broken. I'm going to drop the other piece into my ⌄hand. Has it ⌄broken, Tom? (⌄No, | it ⌄hasn't.)
The piece that dropped to the floor ⌄broke. The piece that dropped into my hand ⌄didn't break, | ⌄did it?

Note that you have used *drop* both transitively and intransitively. This is a common feature of many English verbs. If this is the first example, ask pupils for translations of simple examples (e.g. *I dropped the teapot. The teapot dropped*) to learn whether they have understood. If they have not, give translations yourself.

§ 175. Give further examples, if possible in contexts outside the classroom, and related to local conditions or surroundings. Travel by air may provide examples.

Many people travel by ⌄air now. Planes that cross the At⌄lantic | are usually ⌄large. Planes that fly long ⌄distances | usually have ⌄jet engines. Planes that fly only ⌄short distances | usually have pro⌄pellers.

This sequence includes words (e.g. *jet, propeller*) that may be new. Give the equivalents and do not worry if they are not remembered. Roads and streets may provide further examples. Use the names of roads and streets in your town or district.

You ⁻all know ꜜBridge Street, | ꜜdon't you? It's the street that goes to the ꜜriver. You all know ꜜHigh Street. It's the street that goes through the middle of the ꜜtown.

⁻Do you know the road that goes from here to ꜛX? It's a ꜜwide road, | ꜜisn't it? ⁻Do you know the road that goes to ꜛY? It's a ꜜnarrow road, | ꜜisn't it?

§ **176.** Although the relative *that* (subject) and the finites *is* and *are* are often omitted (as noted in § 174), there are many contexts in which *was* and *were* are not omitted. Give some examples. Put a stress on these finites.

ꜜLook, | there's a ꜜbook on my desk. I'm going to put it on ꜜPaul's desk. There's a book on my ꜜchair, | ꜜtoo. I'm going to put it on ꜜDavid's desk.

⁻Where's the book that ꜜwas /woz/ on my desk? It's on ꜜPaul's desk. ⁻Where's the book that ꜜwas on my chair? It's on ꜜDavid's desk.

§ **177.** When you put questions to the class you want your pupils to use the clauses in their answers. Pupils will probably give short answers. If so, repeat your question and ask for the long and complete answers.

⁻Are the planes that cross the Atlantic usually ꜛlarge? (ꜜYes, | they ꜜare.) ꜜLong answer, please. (ꜜYes, | the planes that cross the Atlantic are usually ꜜlarge.)

Alternative questions:

⁻Is the book that was /woz/[1] on my desk on ꜛPaul's desk now | or on ꜜDavid's desk? (It's on ꜜPaul's desk.) ꜜLong answer, please. (The book that was on your desk is on ꜜPaul's desk now.)

---

[1] Use the strong form /woz/ for contrast.

§ **178.** Next present relative clauses with prepositions. Again use nouns (as antecedents) that are names of things, not persons. Omit the relative *that* (or *which*) and place the preposition after the verb in the clause. Talk about wall pictures or maps, or pictures or photographs that you give to pupils.

I'm looking at a ˅map. The map I'm ⁄looking at | is a map of ˅Asia. I'm looking at a ˅photograph. The photograph I'm ⁄looking at | is a photograph of my ˅father. (*etc., etc.*)

Require pupils to use similar sequences. Give further examples by talking about places.

My brother lives in ˅X. The street he lives in is ˅wide. The house he lives in is ˅small. ⁻Where does our ˅President[1] live? He lives in (˅X). The house he lives in is ˅large. (It's a ˅palace, *etc.*)

With more advanced work it is desirable to get away from a classroom vocabulary and you must use your imagination to find situations and contexts suitable for the items you are presenting.

§ **179.** Next present *who* as the subject of relative clauses. There is no difficulty in finding examples for this, but avoid clauses in which the use of the continuous tenses would make your statements untypical of normal usage. 'The boy who is sitting in the corner' is correct enough, but normally we should shorten this to 'The boy sitting in the corner'. So use the simple, not the continuous, tenses in your first examples.

Tell pupils to perform various momentary activities in turn and then ask questions.

⁻Touch your ˅desk, Tom. ⁻Touch your left ˅elbow, Paul. ⁻Touch your ˅right elbow, David.

⁻Who's the boy who touched his ˅desk? The boy who touched his desk is ˅Tom. ⁻Who's the boy who touched

[1] Or Prime Minister, *etc.*

his left ꝟelbow? The boy who touched his left elbow is
ꝟPaul. ⁻Who's the boy who touched his ꝟright elbow?
The boy who touched his ⁄right elbow | is ꝟDavid.

Give further sequences and require (long) answers from the class.

§ 180. Although 'the boy standing near the door' is preferable to
'the boy *who is* standing near the door' (as noted in the section
above), omissions of this sort with the verb *be* do not occur when the
tense in the clause is Perfect, Past, or Future. Give a few examples.

⁻Who's the boy who has just cleaned the ꝟblackboard?
⁻Who's the boy who was standing at the ꝟdoor a few
moments ago? (*etc.*, *etc.*)

Require long answers to such questions.

§ 181. The object form *whom* is required in formal written style
and in formal speech. In ordinary colloquial style and informal
written style the relative *whom* is usually omitted when it is the
object of the verb, and when it is the object of a preposition.
The man (whom) I saw yesterday . . .
The man I gave the book to . . .
(instead of the more formal: 'The man *to whom* I gave the book').
Here are procedures for presenting this item. Show pictures or
photographs of well-known persons.[1]

⁻Look at these ꝟpictures. This is our (ꝟPresident). This
is our (Prime ꝟMinister). This is ꝟX, | our most famous
(ꝟpoet, *or* ꝟwriter, or inꝟventor).

The man I showed you first is our ꝟPresident. The man
I showed you next is our Prime ꝟMinister. (*etc.*, *etc.*)

⁻Who's the man I showed you ꝟfirst? ꝟLong answer,

---

[1] For *President*, *etc.*, you will substitute whatever titles or names you
think most suitable, or whatever persons for whom pictures or photographs
are available.

please, Paul. (The man you showed us ⌐first | is our ⌐Presi-
dent.) (*etc., etc.*)

After giving further examples write one of your statements on
the blackboard, with *whom* in parentheses, and tell the class that
whom is usually omitted in speech. Repeat your statements and
questions, substituting for 'Who's the man' the words 'What's the
name of the man'.

⌐What's the name of the man I showed you ⌐first? ⌐Long
answer, please, Mary. (The name of the man you showed
us ⌐first | is ⌐X.)

If further examples are needed, tell a number of pupils to stand in
different parts of the classroom.

⌐What's the name of the girl you (can) see at the ⌐black-
board (at the ⌐door, near the ⌐window, in that ⌐corner,
etc.)?

Again require long answers so that pupils use the clause.

§ **182.** Continue with examples in which prepositions occur. Give
various articles to a number of pupils, make statements, and ask
questions.

⌐What's the name of the girl I gave a red ⌐flower to?
The name of the girl I gave a red ⌐flower to | is ⌐Edith.
⌐What's the name of the girl I gave a ⌐white flower to?
(*etc., etc.*)

After this oral presentation write specimen sentences on the
blackboard, with illustrations of the more formal style, and tell
pupils to copy them into their notebooks. Examples:

  ⌠ The man I lent my bicycle to has gone to X.
  ⌡ The man to whom I lent my bicycle has gone to X.
  ⌠ The women he was talking to are French.
  ⌡ The women to whom he was talking are French.

$\begin{cases} \text{The man he works for is a shopkeeper.} \\ \text{The man for whom he works is a shopkeeper.} \end{cases}$

In reading-texts your pupils may find sentences in which the relative *that* is used for persons: 'the people *that* you met yesterday', 'the man *that* I was talking to'. This use is quite correct, but in speech it is much more usual to omit the relative.

§ 183. *Whose* may be dealt with by giving a few examples orally and specimens on the blackboard. Borrow articles from a number of pupils and hold them up in turn. Then make statements.

The name of the boy whose ⌐pen I showed you | is ⌐Paul. The name of the boy whose ⌐book I showed you | is ⌐Charles. (*etc., etc.*)

For blackboard examples:
The man whose bicycle was stolen has gone to the police-station.
Boys whose parents are very poor do not go away during the holidays.

§ 184. When pupils are familiar with relative pronouns they will not have much difficulty with relative adverbs. Instead of long oral presentation and drills it will be sufficient to make a few comments when examples first occur in reading material. Comparisons with relative pronouns are helpful.

$\begin{cases} \text{the house where he lives} \\ \text{the house he lives in (}or\text{ in which he lives)} \end{cases}$
$\begin{cases} \text{the years when I was at school} \\ \text{the years during which I was at school} \end{cases}$
$\begin{cases} \text{the reasons why they sold their house} \\ \text{the reasons for which they sold their house} \end{cases}$

§ 185. There are many other items to be dealt with. Teachers should be on the alert for these and deal with them as they occur. They will be ready to do this if they study the appropriate parts of the books referred to in § 167 above. No attempt should be made to deal with non-defining relative clauses through oral drills. These clauses occur in written English and are best dealt with by means of explanation, followed by written exercises.

EITHER (. . . OR); NEITHER (. . . NOR)
SO (NEITHER, NOR) × A.F. × SUBJECT

§ **186.** In this chapter there are suggestions for presenting a number of structural words which enter into various patterns. These words and patterns are likely to occur in third-year work. They may be dealt with when they occur in reading material. They are all suitable for oral presentation and drills and it is advisable to present them in this way before your pupils see them in print or are required to use them in written work.

§ **187.** *Either . . . or* may be presented in many ways. Here are some procedures suitable for the classroom.
Call a pupil to the blackboard.

I want you to write your ⌄name on the blackboard. Don't write it in the ⌄middle of the blackboard. Write it either in the bottom ⌁right-hand corner | or in the bottom ⌄left-hand corner.

As you speak, point in turn to the two corners. Then hold out two pieces of chalk, one white and the other coloured.

You may use either the ⌁white chalk | or the ⌄red chalk. ⁻Which do you ⌄want?

If there is plenty of time you may put questions:

⁻Where did you (*or* did Tom) write your (*or* his) ⌄name? Did you (*or* he) use the ⌁white chalk | or the ⌄red chalk?

Repeat the sequence with another pupil and with variations, e.g. drawing a cross or a circle, at either the top or the bottom of the blackboard, and with a choice between two other colours. Then call upon one or more pupils to make the statements and requests, and ask questions afterwards.

Another simple procedure is to have an article (e.g. your pen, the duster or eraser for cleaning the blackboard) placed somewhere out of sight, and then talk about it.

ˉWhere's my ↘pen? It's in one of my ↘pockets. It's (*or* It must be) either in ↗this pocket | or in ↘this pocket. ↘Here it is, | in ↘this pocket.

ˉWhere's the ↘duster (e↘raser)? It's either on the ↗ledge, | be↗hind me, | or in this ↘drawer. It isn't on the ↗ledge. It must be in the ↘drawer. ↘Here it is, | in the ↘drawer.

When pupils are to do written work you may say:

You may use either a ↗pen | or a ↘pencil. You may write either in ↗ink | or in ↘pencil.

This use of *in* may need comment. *In pencil* (no article) indicates the material, not the article, and may be compared with 'a statue *in marble* (*wood, etc.*)'.

Use any other opportunities that occur for occasional use of the new item.

I shall give you a ↘test next week, | either on ↗Tuesday | or ↘Wednesday.

ˉWhat's the ↘date? It's either the ↗fifth | or the ↘sixth, | ↗isn't it?[1]

§ **188.** A less frequent use of *either* is for 'one or the other'. When *either* occurs in this sense, give two or three examples.

ˉAsk me for a ↘ball, John. (ˉPlease give me a ↘ball.) Here are ↘two balls. Take ↘either of them.

---

[1] Rise in pitch on *isn't* because you are pretending to be uncertain and you want an answer.

ˉCome to the ↘blackboard, Paul, | and ˉwrite the word ↘*green*. ˉWrite it on ↘either side of the board, | ↗left | or ↘right.

Another use of *either* is 'each of two'. This, too, is comparatively infrequent, and *both* is much commoner. When it occurs, give one or two examples and compare the use of *both*.

There are shops on ˉeither side (on ˉboth sides) of the ↘street.

There are curtains on ˉeither side (on ˉboth sides) of the ↘window.

§ 189. Here are suggestions for presenting *neither . . . nor*.

ˉWhere's my ↘book? Is it on my ↗desk. (↘No, | it ↘isn't.) Is it on ↗your desk? (↘No, | it ↘isn't.) It's neither on ↗my desk | nor on ↘yours. It's in this ↘drawer (↘bag, *etc.*).[1]

ˉWhat colour is this (↘book)? It's neither ↗yellow | nor ↘brown, | ↘is it? It's ↘khaki.

ˉWhat kind of ↘fruit is there in the shops now? Are there any (↗apples)? (↘No, | there ↘aren't.) Are there any (↗oranges)? (↘No, | there ↘aren't.) There are neither (↗apples) | nor (↘oranges) in the shops now.[2]

Have ˉyou ever been to (↗X), Paul? (↘No, | I ↘haven't.) Have you ˉever been to (↗Y)? (↘No, | I ↘haven't.) Paul has been to neither (↗X) | nor to (↘Y)?[3] Have ↗you ever been

[1] Do not allow pupils to see where the book is in advance. You do not want the answer 'No, it's in your drawer'.

[2] Use the names of any kinds of fruit (or other articles of food) that are out of season.

[3] Give names of places which pupils are very unlikely to have visited.

to X, Peter? (ˎNo, | I ˎhaven't.) Neither ˏPaul | nor ˎPeter has ever been to X.

§ **190.** When other uses of *neither* occur in reading material, give a few extra examples.

I've drawn ˉtwo ˎcats on the blackboard. ˎNeither drawing is very good, | ˎis it? ˎNeither of them is very good. They're ˉboth ˎbad drawings.

ˉStand ˎup, Tom. ˉIs Tom a ˏtall boy? (ˎNo, | he ˎisn't.) ˎHarry, | ˎyou stand up, please. Is ˏHarry a tall boy? (ˎNo, | he ˎisn't.) Neither ˉTom nor ˎHarry is tall. They're ˉboth ˎshort.

ˉHow far is (ˎX) from here? It's about (ˉfive ˎmiles.) ˉHow far is (ˎY) from here?[1] It's about (ˎthree miles). Neither (ˉX) nor (ˎY) is very far from here. ˎNeither of these places is far from here. ˎNeither town (*or* village) is far from here.

§ **191.** A commonly used pattern in which *so* and *neither* (or *nor*) occur is that in which *so* or *neither* is followed by one of the twenty-four anomalous finites and the subject, as in 'So am I', 'So does he', 'Neither did you', 'Nor did my brother'. When examples occur in reading material oral presentation and drills will be useful.

Note that in this pattern there is a fall in pitch at the end. The anomalous finite is unstressed, so that weak form is used. It is important, therefore, that pupils should hear numerous examples. Here are specimens, with phonemic transcriptions, to illustrate these weak forms.

So am I	/sou əm ˎai./
So does my brother.	/sou dəz mai ˎbrʌðə./
So shall I.	/sou ʃ(ə)l ˎai./

[1] Give names of places that are not far away.

Note that the two words *so shall* in the last examples are pronounced like the word *social* /ˈsouʃəl/ or /ˈsouʃl/.

| Nor has anyone. | /nɔ: həz ꜜeniwʌn./ |
| Neither can you. | /naiðə kən ꜜju:./ |

§ **192.** Suggestions for presenting this pattern follow. Start with *so*, using statements with *too*.

You ⁻all came to ꜛschool this morning. ꜛI came to school this morning, | ꜛtoo.

Note the steep fall in pitch on *I* in the second statement. This fall is repeated in the re-statement that follows.

You will ⁻all come to school to ꜛmorrow.[1] ꜛI shall come to school tomorrow, | ꜛtoo.

You'll ⁻all come to school to ꜛmorrow. So shall ꜛI. /sou ʃəl ꜜai./

Do ⁻you like ↗oranges, Tom? (ꜜYes, | I ꜜdo.) Do ↗you like oranges, | ↗too, Peter? (ꜜYes, | I ꜜdo.) ↗Tom likes oranges, | and ⁻so does ꜛPeter. /ənd ⁻sou dəz ꜜpi:tə./

Have ⁻you a ↗pen, John? (ꜜYes, | I ꜜhave.) Have ↗you a pen, Charles? (ꜜYes, | I ꜜhave.)

↗John has a pen, | and ⁻so has ꜛCharles. |ənd ⁻sou həz ꜛtʃa:lz./ ↗John and Charles have pens, | and ⁻so have ꜛI. /ənd ⁻sou həv ꜜai./

Can ⁻you ↗swim, Paul? (ꜜYes, | I ꜜcan.) Can ↗you swim, George? (ꜜYes, | I ꜜcan.)

↗Paul can swim, | and ⁻so can ꜛGeorge. /ənd ⁻sou kən ꜜdʒɔ:dʒ./

You will find it easy to provide further examples. Use a variety of finite verbs in the pattern: *am, is, are, was, were; have, has, had;*

---

[1] Or *on* ꜛ*Monday* (*etc.*) if the following day is one with no school.

do, does, did; will, shall; can, could; possibly *must.* You need not at present provide examples of *would* and *should, need, may, ought.* These are less important.

§ **193.** When pupils have heard a large number of examples, tell your pupils that you now want them to use the pattern. You, or your pupils in turn, will make simple statements. Pupils will then make a statement using *so.* The first statement must, of course, be affirmative.

Teacher:	I have a ∨pen.	(∕Tom ?)
Tom:	So have ∨I.	
Teacher:	I like ∨oranges.	(∕Peter ?)
Peter:	So do ∨I.	
Teacher:	I can ∨swim.	(∕Paul ?)
Paul:	So can ∨I.	

After this drill in which the pupils use *I*, tell the class to use, instead of *I*, the name of a classmate, or the names of two classmates.

Teacher:	Tom has a ⁻green ∨book.	(∕Peter ?)
Peter:	So has ∨Paul. (*or*) So have Paul and ∨Charles.	
Teacher:	John can ∨swim.	(∕Ralph ?)
Ralph:	So can ∨Dick. (*or*) So can Dick and ∨Derek.	
Teacher:	Frank will come to school to∨morrow.	
		(∕Arthur ?)
Arthur:	So will ∨Andrew. (*or*) So will Andrew and ∨Brian.	

This drill may need time and patience before pupils understand what you want from them, but actual use of the new pattern is more important and useful than a mere theoretical understanding of the word-order.

§ **194.** When the pattern with *so* is mastered, present examples with *neither* and *nor.* Make two negative statements. Combine them

with *neither . . . nor*. Then present the pattern: *neither* (or *nor*) ×
finite verb × subject.

You ⁻haven't been to ˅Paris, | ˅have you, Paul?[1] ˅You
haven't been to Paris, | ˅have you, Peter? Neither ⁻Paul
nor ˅Peter has been to Paris.

/Paul hasn't been to Paris, | and ⁻neither has ˅Peter.
/Paul hasn't been to Paris. | ⁻Nor has ˅Peter.

Tell the class that both *neither* and *nor* are used in this pattern.

You ⁻can't speak ˅Russian, George, | ˅can you? ˅You
can't speak Russian, | ˅can you, Ralph? Neither ⁻George
nor ˅Ralph can speak Russian. /George can't speak
Russian, | and ⁻neither can ˅Ralph.

The last sequence may be used again with *don't* and *do* in the first
statements, and with *does(n't)* in the statements that follow.

You ⁻don't speak ˅Spanish, Mary, | ˅do you? ˅You
don't speak Spanish, Betty, | ˅do you? Neither /Mary | nor
˅Betty speaks Spanish. /Mary doesn't speak Spanish; |
⁻neither does ˅Betty.

Instead of 'neither does Betty', it is possible to say:

˅Betty doesn't speak Spanish, | ˅either.

Do not confuse pupils by using this variation at present. Later on,
when recalling and practising this pattern, give examples of the
variation.

§ 195. After giving examples with the chief finites (as for *so* in
§ 192 above), require pupils to use the pattern with *neither* or *nor*.
Use the procedures suggested for *so* in § 193 above.

For further practice written exercises are useful. Provide a number
of pairs of sentences and require pupils to convert the second of each

---

[1] Fall in pitch on *have* because you know that the answer is 'No'.

pair into a sentence that begins with *so, neither* or *nor*. Written exercises make possible a wider variety of subject matter. Here are models:

John has a new bicycle. His brother has a new bicycle, too.

Answer: So has his brother.

Mr and Mrs Green went (will go, have been, *etc.*) to Japan. Mr and Mrs Brown went (will go, have been, *etc.*) to Japan, too.

Answer: So did (will, have) Mr and Mrs Brown.

Mary doesn't like cheese. Joan doesn't like cheese, either.

Answer: Neither (*or* Nor) does Joan.

EACH (OTHER); EVERY, ALL;
EVERY OTHER
SOME/OTHERS; ALL/BOTH; ELSE
THE EMPHATIC PRONOUNS

§ **196.** *Each, other, every, some, all* and *both* are words of high frequency. Your pupils have, at this stage, certainly met and used them. They are structural words which have to be learnt not in isolation but in patterns and collocations. In this chapter there are suggestions for dealing with some of these which have not so far been treated.

§ **197.** *Each* must be clearly distinguished from *every. Each* has the idea of 'one by one' or 'separately'. Start with *every* and *all* and then use *each* in contexts that show the difference.

ˉHow many boys (girls) are there in this ˅class? There are (˅thirty). Have ˉall of you (got) ⁄books? ˅Yes, | ˉall of you have (got) ˅books. You ˉall have ˅books. ˉEvery boy (girl) in this class has a ˅book.

˅Tom, | ˅Dick, | ˅Harry, | ˉcome to my ˅desk, please. I'm going to give ˉeach of you a ˅ball. ˉWhat have I ˅given you, Tom? (You've given me a ˅ball.) ˉWhat have I given ˅you, Dick? (You've given ˅me a ball, | ˅too.) ˉHave I given ⁄you a ball, Harry? (˅Yes, | you ˅have.)

ˉWhat did I ˅do, | a minute a˅go? I gave ˉeach of you a ˅ball. Then I asked ˉeach of you a ˅question. ˉEach of you ˅answered my question.

ˉDid I ask ⁄each of you a question, Tom, | or did I ask only ˅you a question? (You asked ˅each of us a question.)

Write on the blackboard:

{ I gave each boy a ball.
{ I gave each of the boys a ball.
{ Everybody in this class has a pen.
{ All the boys in this class have books.

§ **198.** Give examples of *each* and *both*. Call out two pupils.

⁻Come ↘here, Paul. ⁻Stand on my ↘right, please. ↘Peter, | ⁻come and stand ↘here, | on my ↘left.

I have a boy on ⁻each ↘side of me. Paul's on my ↗right, | and ⁻Peter's on my ↘left. You may ⁻go back to your ↘seats.

⁻What have I in my right ↘hand, Tom? (You have a ↘ball.) ⁻What have I in my ↘left hand, Arthur? (You have a ball in your ↘left hand, | ↘too.) I have a ball in ⁻each ↘hand.

Now take up something large, using both hands.

⁻What have I in my hands ↘now? I have a ⁻large ↘box. I'm holding it in ⁻both ↘hands. It's too ↘large to hold in ↗one hand.

§ **199.** *Every other* has two meanings. It may mean 'all the others' and it may mean 'alternate'. Do not give these two meanings together. Deal with each when there are examples in reading material.

Draw a number of short lines on the blackboard, one of them different in some way from the rest.

⁻Look at the ↘blackboard. These are ↘lines, | ↘aren't they? ⁻Look at ↘this line. It's ↘red. All the ↗other lines | are ↘white. There's ⁻one ↘red line. Every ⁻other line is ↘white.

⁻Look at the blackboard a↘gain. These are ↘words. This word is a ↘French word.[1] All the ⁻other words are ↘English

---

[1] Or a word from the language of your pupils.

words. There's ⁻one ↘French word. Every ↗other word | is
↘English.

§ **200.** When examples of *every other* meaning 'alternate' occur
in reading material, give two or three other examples.

⁻Look at these lines on the ↘blackboard. I'm going to
rub some of them ↘out. I'm rubbing out the ↘first line.
Now I'm rubbing out the ↘third line. I've rubbed out the
↘fifth line. (*etc., etc.*)
I've rubbed out ⁻every other ↘line.

Another example may be given by using a wall calendar.

Mr X went to the cinema ⁻very ↘often last month. He
went on the ↗first of (May), | on the ↗third, | on the ↗fifth, |
on the ↗seventh. (*etc., etc.*)
He went to the cinema ⁻every other ↘day.

§ **201.** The contrast between *some of* (*the books, etc.*) and *the
others* was dealt with in *Stage Two*, § 140. The use of *others* without
the definite article needs to be presented. When this use first occurs
in reading material the procedures given here may be useful. Place
several piles of books (or other articles), one pile on your desk and
other piles on the desk of a pupil, on a chair or table, *etc.*

↘Look, | there are some /ðərəsəm/ ↘books on my desk.
There are ⁻others on the ↘chair. There are ⁻others on the
↘floor. There are ⁻others on that ↘table. There are ⁻others
on Tom's ↘desk.

When there is a definite contrast, *some* has the strong form /sʌm/.
This may be presented by means of examples such as these:

⁻Some /sʌm/ people ↘like travelling by air. Others ↘don't.
They like to travel by ↘sea, | or by ↘rail.

Some people like going to ⌄foreign countries for their holidays. Others like their ⌄own country for holidays.

⁻What kinds of ⌄fruit are there in the shops now? Some kinds are ex⌄pensive, | ⌄aren't they? Others ⌄aren't expensive; | they're ⌄cheap.

Some boys (girls) learn English ⌄quickly. Others ⌄don't learn quickly.

§ 202. The reciprocal pronouns *each other* and *one another* may usefully be illustrated with further examples when they occur in reading material. Do not tell your pupils that *each other* is restricted to two persons or things and that *one another* is used for more than two. This is a mistaken (though harmless) belief, not in accordance with usage.

Here are suggestions for presenting these items.

⌄John, | ⁻look at ⌄Peter. ⌄Peter, | ⁻look at ⌄John. ⁻What are John and Peter ⌄doing? They're ⌄looking at each other. ⁻What are you and Peter ⌄doing, John? (We're ⌄looking at each other.)

⁻How many boys (girls) are there in this ⌄class? There are (⌄thirty,) | ⌄aren't there? ⁻Do you all ∕know each other? ⌄Yes, | you ⌄do. ⁻Each of you knows all the ⌄others. You ⁻know each other ⌄well. You ⁻see each other (*or* one another) every ⌄day.

Give an example with *'s*.

You know each other's (*or* one another's) ⌄names, | ⌄don't you?

§ 203. *All* and *both* are already known to your pupils in their most usual patterns.[1] Pupils may not have heard or seen many examples of

---

[1] See *Stage One*, §§ 153–155, and *Stage Two*, §§ 18–21.

the pattern in which *all* and *both* are used in apposition. When you need to present and drill this new item start by recalling what has already been dealt with and then introduce the new usage.

˹Look at these ˎbooks. ˹All of these books are ˎmine. These books are ˹all ˎmine. These books ˹all belong to ˎme.

˹Look at these two ˎpens. Both of these ˎpens are mine. These pens are ˹both ˎmine. These pens ˹both belong to ˎme.

ˎMary, | ˎSusan, | ˹go to the ˎdoor, please. ˹Both girls are walking to the ˎdoor. ˹Both girls are now standing at the ˎdoor. They ˹both went to the door a few seconds aˎgo. They're ˹both at the ˎdoor now.

§ **204.** The position of *all* and *both* when in apposition is worth commenting on to your pupils. These two words, like some adverbs of frequency (e.g. *often*, *never*) follow the common anomalous finites (*are*, *were*, *have*, etc.), but precede non-anomalous finites. Write on the blackboard, for pupils to copy into their notebooks:

{ These books *are all* mine.
{ These books *all belong* to me.
{ The girls *are both* at the door.
{ The girls *both went* to the door.
{ He *has often* (*never*) been to Europe.
{ He *often* (*never*) *goes* to Europe.

Call attention to the position of *all* and *both* in the first two pairs and compare the position of *often* (*never*) in the third pair. Repeat the sequences used above (in § 203) with variations and require pupils to answer questions so that they use *all* and *both* in apposition. Ask alternative questions. (Simple 'Yes' and 'No' questions would receive short answers only.)

ˉAre these books ⌐all mine | or are some of them ˅yours? (Those books are ˉall ˅yours.)

ˉDo these books ⌐both belong to Tom | or does one of them belong to ˅you, John? (Those books ˉboth belong to ˅Tom.) (*etc., etc.*)

§ 205. *Else* is an adverb closely linked to the pronouns *what, who, something, anything, nothing, somebody, anybody, nobody* and the adverb *where*. Suggestions for presenting it orally follow. Talk about articles on your desk, and in a box (or bag).

There are some ˅books on my desk. ˉWhat ˅else is there on my desk? There's a ˅box. ˉWhat ˅else is there on my desk? ˉWhat ˅else can you see on my desk, Charles? (I can see a ˅bag.) ˉDo you know what there is in the ⌐box, John? (˅No, | I ˅don't.) ˅Look, | there's a ˅ball. ˉIs there anything ⌐else in the box? ˅Yes, | there's something ˅else; | there's a ˅bottle. ˉIs there anything ⌐else. ˅Yes, | there's a piece of ˅wood. Is there anything ⌐else in the box? ˅No. | there's ˉnothing ˅else. The box is ˅empty now.

Repeat by asking and answering questions about the contents of the bag. Then repeat the three sequences (the articles on the desk, in the box, and in the bag) and, when pupils show by answering that they understand the use of *else*, require pupils to come forward and repeat your sequences. Change the articles on the desk, and in the box and bag, for variety.

§ 206. For *who, somebody*, etc., call upon pupils to go and stand somewhere in the room.

ˉGo and stand near the ˅door, Tom. ˉYou, ˅too, John. ˉIs Tom near the ⌐door, David? (˅Yes, | he ˅is.) ˉWho ˅else is near the door? (˅John is.) ˉIs anybody ⌐else standing near the door? ꜛNo, | ꜛnobody else is standing there.

Tell two other pupils to stand in a corner of the room.

˜Is Paul standing in that ⸝corner? (ꜛYes, | he ꜛis.) There's somebody ꜛelse in that corner. ˜Who ꜛis it, John? (It's ꜛPeter.)

Note the use of *it* for a person not yet named. You may need to comment on this. Say that *he* and *she* are used for persons already referred to or identified. Example:

˜Who's at the ꜛdoor? It's the ꜛpostman. He's brought a ꜛparcel for you.

Repeat these and other sequences and require answers from the class. Require pupils to use the sequences.

To illustrate the use of the possessive you may show a pencil or other article that you may have found (or that you pretend to have found), and say:

˜This pencil isn't ꜛmine; it's somebody ꜛelse's /elsiz/ pencil. ˜Whose ꜛis it?

§ 207. The use of *else* with *where* may be presented by talking about places which you or your pupils have or have not visited.

I went to (ꜛX) last month (summer, year, *etc*.). I went to (ꜛY), | ꜛtoo, | and I went to (ꜛZ). I ˜didn't go to any ꜛother place. I went ˜nowhere ꜛelse.

˜Where did ꜛyou go last month, John? (I went to ꜛ . . . .) ˜Where ꜛelse did you go?

Another procedure is to place a number of articles in various places in the classroom, some easily seen and some out of sight.

ꜛLook, | there's a ꜛball on my desk. ˜Can you see any

ʃmore balls in this room? There's one on the ˅floor, | in that ˅corner. There's one somewhere ˅else. Can /kən/ ‾anyone see anʃother ball? There's another ball on the floor in ˅this corner.

§ 208. The Reflexive Pronouns were dealt with in *Stage Two*, Chapter Fifteen, so your pupils are familiar with the forms *myself*, *ourselves*, *himself*, *herself*, *themselves*, *etc.* The use of these pronouns for emphasis may be dealt with when examples occur in reading material. Suggestions for presenting these uses and for oral drills follow.

§ 209. The alternative positions of the pronoun needs to be illustrated. Ask a number of pupils to perform some kind of activity in turn. Ask and answer questions after the pupils have performed the activities.

‾Come to my ˅desk, John. ‾Pick up this ˅book. ‾Put it on ˅Tom's desk. ‾Now put it back on ˅my desk.

‾What did John ˅do, | a few ˅seconds ago? He ‾picked up this ˅book. He put it on ˅Tom's desk. Then he put it back on ˅my desk.

Then perform the actions yourself. In your first statements place the emphatic pronoun after the subject of each sentence.

I my˅self am going to pick up the book. I my˅self am going to put it on Tom's desk. I my˅self am going to put it back on my desk.

When you have performed the activities, repeat your statements. This time make double statements placing the emphatic pronoun first at the end and then after the subject.

‾Did ʃJohn pick up that book a few seconds ago? ˅No, | he ˅didn't. I picked it up my˅self. I my˅self picked it up. ‾Did ʃJohn put it on Tom's desk? ˅No, | he ˅didn't.

I put it on Tom's desk my˅self. I my˅self put it on Tom's
desk. ˉWho put it back on ˅my desk? (˅You did.) ˅Yes, | I
put it back on my desk my˅self. I my˅self put it back on
my desk.

Note the steep fall in pitch on the syllable -*self* in these examples.
This is advisable here to give prominence to the idea of emphasis.
Note also the inclusion, in this sequence, of the question 'Did John
pick up that book (put it on John's desk, put it back . . .)? This is
advisable to make clear the contrast between the first series of
activities and the second, on which emphasis is to be placed.

Give other sequences (e.g. going to the window, breaking a
piece of chalk). Require pupils to answer the questions. Require
pairs of pupils to go through similar sequences while you stand by
and listen.

§ 210. Give examples in which the other emphatic pronouns are
used: *himself, herself, yourself, yourselves, themselves.* Alternative
questions may be used to ensure that pupils use the new forms in
their answers.

ˉDid Mary her˄self open the door (*or* open the door
her˄self) | or did ˅you open the door? (Mary her˅self
opened the door.) (*or* Mary opened the door her˅self.)

§ 211. Give examples with intransitive verbs.

ˉDid Tom him˄self go to the blackboard | or did he ask
˅John to go there?

ˉDid you your˄self go out of the room | or did you ask
˅Jane to go out? (I my˅self went out of the room.)

Sequences of this kind are easily provided. You have only to
make suitable requests and then ask alternative questions.

§ 212. The emphatic pronoun may refer to the object of the verb.
In this case it is placed after the object. Examples may be given (and
written on the blackboard, to be copied into notebooks).

I saw (spoke to) Mr Green himself (not his wife, secretary, *etc.*).

Cf. { I myself saw Mr Green.
    { (*or*) I saw Mr Green myself.

Translation will help here.

I saw (spoke to) the players themselves.

Cf. { I myself saw the players.
    { I saw the players myself.

§ 213. When these pronouns are used with the preposition *by,* the meaning may be 'alone'. Suggestions for presenting this item follow.

ˎJohn, | ˉgo and stand in that ˎcorner (*or* at the ˎdoor).

ˉIs there anyone in the corner with ˏJohn? ˎNo, | he's standing there by himˎself. He's aˎlone. You're standing there by yourˎself, John. You're aˎlone.

§ 214. Another meaning is 'alone and without help'. This is easy to demonstrate.

ˉCan you lift this book-case by yourˏself, Tom? ˎTry. ˎNo, | you ˎcan't. You ˉcan't lift it by yourˎself. You ˉcan't lift it aˎlone.

Use this situation to recall *could* and the preposition *without* and to present *help* as a noun.

ˎPaul, | ˉhelp Tom to lift the ˎbook-case. ˉDid Tom and Paul lift the book-case toˏgether? ˎYes, | they ˎdid. Tom ˉcouldn't lift the book-case by himˎself. He ˉcouldn't lift it aˎlone. He ˉcouldn't lift it without ˎhelp. When Paul ˏhelped him | he ˎcould lift it.

Repeat these sequences, and use similar sequences, requiring answers from the class. Use these pronouns incidentally whenever there are opportunities, for example by asking about homework or travel.

˜Did you do your homework by your↗self, | or did somebody ↘help you?

˜Did you go to (X) by your↗self (a↗lone), | or did your brother (sister, father, *etc.*) go ↘with you?

§ 215. The use of *all* before *myself, etc.*, gives additional emphasis. *All* in such cases means 'quite'. Give examples.

I did this work ˜all by my↘self.[1]
We're ˜all by our↘selves.[2]

[1] i.e. without any help at all; quite alone.
[2] i.e. with no other persons present; quite alone.

CUMULATIVE INDEX OF STRUCTURAL AND 'HEAVY DUTY' WORDS

I = Stage One; II = Stage Two; III = Stage Three

NOTE: If a section number is marked with an asterisk, it indicates that the word is used only incidentally at this point, and is (or will be) dealt with in greater detail later.